What's In It For You?

You should simply consider, essential math. Suppose you submit just ten dollars per week in fake or swelled costs. That is $520 per year in tracked down cash to you.

Better yet, this cash is, by law, tax exempt. By the principles of the IRS, genuine operational expense caused by a worker over the span of ordinary business, are repaid without affecting that representative's available status. At the end of the day, it isn't pay. In principle, there is no net advantage to the employee.

The standards in this book are in opposition to these guidelines. If you just spend
$200, however gather $300 from your boss from a cushioned cost report, you're getting $100 in additional pay. On the off chance that the IRS had some awareness of it, they'd need to burden it. Help us hard and fast and don't tell them.

If you live in an assessment section, as most working class individuals, where the public authority takes around 40% of your cash to reallocate the riches, your $520 of additional costs, approaches more like $870 of gross income.

Indeed, when you consider federal retirement aide charge, Medicare charge, state handicap charge, and other nearby expenses; there's a great deal of you out there losing fifty pennies on the dollar to the public authority. Thus, every additional dollar you can get compensated on a cost report to you, really implies two dollars in your pocket.

Now check out the different. Assuming that you're in a position where you could average $100 every week in bogus costs, you help your salary by $5200 per year, which is a pre-charge salary increase of $8700.

And assuming you are one of those chiefs (I know somewhere around one of you is understanding this) who could stow away $500 per week in additional costs, the net money in your pocket is about $26,000, which implies you singularly gave yourself no less than a $43,000 raise.

I don't be aware of you, yet I could generally discover a few use for a couple of additional bucks for nothing. Simply recollect, this is notwithstanding every one of the authentic advantages business ledgers can bring you. With the preferred customer credits, the free evenings in inns, the suppers for you and companions, and free lawful and monetary exhortation you get, your genuine pay is altogether bigger than the gross number you see on your own check stub.

How Do I Justify It?

Actually, I've been doing it and pulling off it for such a long time, I don't stress over it any more. The greater part of the little deceives I will show you have become natural, it feels normal. Assuming you will do this, they better become natural to you. The more normal these become, the more acceptable you will show up on the uncommon events you are approached to clarify what you did.

When I really do stress over it however, I first glance by any means of the benefits my organization makes and the brutal things they will do to make them. Assuming that the organization needs to make their primary concern by laying off 100 laborers, you can wager they don't lose any rest over it. They are not worried about the children whose fathers or moms don't really have jobs.

Second, I check out a portion of the profane compensations the leaders make.

How is it that in a year where a car company loses a billion dollars, the CEO gets a million dollar bonus? How is it that an airline can ask for pay concessions from their workers to make ends meet, and then have the board of directors fly to the Bahamas for a meeting where they vote themselves a big pay raise? They watch out for their own, so why shouldn't I?

Third, what most laborers shouldn't don't have a clue, are simply the advantages upper administration give. They aren't recorded anyplace. They're only one of those "gracious coincidentally" sort of things. Normally they start at the VP level. They provide themselves with the little honor of utilizing one of the organization vehicles, or restrictive utilization of an organization fitness center, or participations at greens, or season passes to pro athletics. When there are investment opportunities to pass around, they take the overwhelming majority and pass along the small still needs to be shared by a higher degree of the executives. They legitimize it utilizing my fourth reason.

I am salaried, which implies I get a similar measure of cash consistently in my check paying little heed to how long I work. This ordinarily is an alluring idea, in that you dream you can come in at nine and leave at four, aside from Wednesday evening when you golf. That main works for the first class in the partnership. You observe they need you to work longer hours for the equivalent dollars.

When you are salaried, you first observe you are approached to fly on Sunday so you are there for a Monday early daytime meeting. You are approached to surrender a Saturday so the organization can diminish airfare with the Saturday night stay.

When the organization must have somebody stay late for some undertaking, you get to remain in light of the fact that they would need to compensate double time to the hourly laborers. To the organization, you are free, read in "slave", labor.

All of the individual time you spend flying for the organization, going through evenings out and about in lodgings, and all of the driving time you spend in the driver's seat is lost time. Cushioning your costs to get a couple of additional bucks, is as yet a can foresee the organization and some pitiful pay to you.

I would rather not sound harsh, however one thing I have discovered the most difficult way, is that you are extra assuming it suits the organization's necessities. The organization, and the on going presence of the key leaders, comes first.

Have you at any point considered what truly continues in a corporate consolidation? It's a great deal like sand part ball games. One of the two organization pioneers gets their thumb on the handle of the bat. They will pick the principal corporate official who will remain with the organization. Then the other CEO picks their choice, and so on down the line. I accept that I'm the ungraceful, nearsighted nerd who will be picked last.

As the waste material runs down the slope, each degree of the board inquires, "Who would I be able to give the shaft to, to save my butt." They got are as yet getting "theirs", and they will secure it no matter what. I know whether it secures their position, they will dump me like a hot potato , so I figure, I will get my part of the pie while I can.

I've been "down estimated" twce in my profession and it isn't entertaining. You give long stretches of die hard loyalty to your organization, with practically no dark imprints on your record and a lot of achievements to note. At some point, your organization decides the little box on the hierarchical diagram with your name in it, is no longer needed.

Your supervisor calls you in and gives you an all around pre-arranged check and tells you, "Please accept my apologies, it's not all that much, yet you're being laid off. You've accomplished incredible work for ourselves as well as it's a disgrace, however such is reality in the enormous corporate world."

In additional conversations, you discover it doesn't truly has anything to do with you or the task you've finished. They required the decrease in head count, and your case is superfluous. No conversation of different regions for you to work, simply great bye.

Well, I'm sorry as well. It's not all that much, yet assuming I can be kicked out the entryway for doing nothing out of sorts, for what reason would it be a good idea for me I stress over a couple of additional bucks taken from the organization's coffers?

The Business Philosophy of Expenses

This might sound insane to some of you, however organizations really need costs. Without a doubt, they don't need such a large number of them, yet they need them. In a few business circumstances, especially deals, your bosses might even think you are not doing your work assuming you don't spend enough on entertaining.

The old "three martini lunch" is the thing that makes the business world go round. It might have been supplanted with horse feed sprout sandwiches and mineral water, yet the business lunch charged to someone's organization is the oil which keeps the cog wheels of industry turning.

The thinking is really a similar one used to legitimize cushioning your cost report. Contingent upon how a company is organized, their duty sections can be higher than yours. The thing that matters is partnerships pay charges on "benefits" not income.

Legitimate operational expense are "counterbalances" against benefits. Each dollar spent on costs conceals a dollar of benefits from the IRS. Consequently, every dollar they spend on authentic costs acquires them fifty pennies of undetectable profits.

This rationale is most frequently utilized by bookkeepers in what is known as the gathering technique for accounting. Toward the finish of every month, quarter, or year the organization gathers for "expected" costs which could conceivably really appear next quarter.

If the organization gets around the year's end and there looks as though there will be a duty responsibility, they will build as many "likely" costs as they can. Anything which seems as though it very well may be paid in the following year, will be "accumulated" for the current year, so that on paper they owe less in taxes.

If these costs never really emerge, they'll simply delay until the following year's results to see what to do. Authoritatively, bookkeepers utilize this to "level" the ups and down of the financial thrill ride. At vital occasions, it is utilized to

confound the duty collectors.

In the vast majority of my occupations I have been urged to spend the organization 's cash. I put in a couple of years as a Sales Manager, controlling the endeavors of fifteen salespeople. On the off chance that I wasn't accepting meals and paying for golf excursions for clients, my supervisor would really stroll into my office and inquire, "What the heck aren't you doing out there?"

My manager genuine dreaded "different folks" around were purchasing everybody better snacks, so assuming we didn't, we'd lose the business. My manager thought rivals were offering more and preferable gifts over I was.

Exactly the same thing streamed down to my salespeople. I had two who were similarly effective, over-accomplishing their objectives by about a similar rate. One had gigantic cost reports consistently, with golf trips one time each week and snacks consistently. The other would have one 10th how much expenses.

Mind you, both were pounding their numbers by comparative sums, and rationale would make you think, "Assuming I can have similar incomes coming in for one 10th how much costs, that is something to be thankful for." Not in the business world. My supervisor inspected the costs for salesmen and her impression was the primary rep was in effect "more dynamic and involved", and got more acclaim and grants that the last option. Go figure.

Record Keeping and Your Boss's Oversight

The genuine mystery of cushioning your cost report and pulling off it is documentation. As a matter of fact, the more precise word would be over documentation. The more data you give, the more real your report will appear.

People typically believe being ambiguous and trusting your manager will disregard the cost, is the best strategy, as it leaves you more "leeway" when it comes time to clarify. They feel that falling back upon "I can't recall" will work constantly. It doesn't work.

Just consider it. On the off chance that you can easily forget significant subtleties, how astute would you say you are? Assuming you can't recall who you ate with, how might they entrust you with genuine responsibility?

Stand by your costs gladly and certainly. Your manager is more averse to address them. In the event that the supervisor asks, clarify them serenely and definitely.

Put your manager on the spot by offering something like, "Did I not comprehend the cost strategy correctly?"

The truth of the matter is, your manager would rather not invest a great deal of energy perusing and

endorsing cost reports. OK, so there are a couple of exacting sorts out there who utilize a magnifying lens to look at reports, however they are rare.

Most managers will go through under thirty seconds examining a cost report. Most really depend on their secretaries or clerical specialists. A chief making sixty dollars and hour, can't squander ten minutes ($10) to track down a three dollar disparity. Duplicate this by anyway many reports they manage consistently, and they truly don't have any desire to bother.

The secretary is a lot gentler touch. In the first place, most secretaries or clerical specialists, try to avoid the manner in which they are treated by their chief, so doing the "manager's work" by evaluating reports, isn't one of their beloved errands either.

Most secretaries are come up short on and exhausted. They typically possibly have the opportunity to check whether every thing is upheld by a receipt. Assuming there is a receipt for every passage and a clarification for the cost which appears to be sensible, they'll endorse it or advise the manager to support it without being questioned.

You can help your possibilities on the off chance that you are great to the secretary. On the off chance that you realize they are an essential reviewer, propose to take care of them. Put in no time flat to inquire, "Am I giving you all that you want on those cost reports? Is there anything I can do to make it simpler for you to deal with my cost report?"

Thank the secretary for turning the reports around rapidly. You tell them, "These operational expense make my energize card charges construct so quick, and your handling my reports rapidly helps keep me out of a monetary tie. I'm certain you can sympathize."

The secretary sees your costs and undoubtedly is astounded you can deal with them. Most operational expense would seriously affect most secretaries on what they're paid. What you truly are expressing to her however is, "A debt of gratitude is in order for not looking too carefully at my expenses."

As another clue, it truly wouldn't damage to purchase the secretary lunch (Hide it on your cost report?) or get them a little gift some an ideal opportunity for the difficult work they are doing to assist you with cost reports. A smidgen of generosity can purchase a major measure of leeway.

I'll cover a significant part of the documentation issues inside ensuing sections and where they will all the more straightforwardly relate to circumstances. It is significant, notwithstanding, to understand the critical piece of documentation is the receipt. Receipts come in all shapes and sizes. Receipts can be acquired from many sources and in numerous ways, not really by really bringing about the expense.

The nearby office supply store needs to turn into your companion. The stockroom kind of office provider can turn into your absolute best companion. Organizations purchase receipt materials some place. Would you be able to think about where? You got it. The workplace supply store.

The essential café request books with the tearoff receipt at the base are accessible in stack of fifty, ten cushions to the bundle for under ten bucks. They are accessible in many plans, shadings, and sizes. If you buy a few different kinds, you'll have a lifetime supply of receipts.

An expression of caution here. Generally every one of them have chronic numbers at the base for interior controls by the café. Ensure you pivot arbitrarily through the numbers. Consecutive receipt numbers on a cost report would be a dead give away.

Mastercard and Visa slips are likewise accessible in different organizations at the workplace provider. Contingent on how modern you need to be, engraving machines can be purchased, and the engraving plates can be requested. In many states, no verification of a real business is needed to arrange a plate for the engraving machine.

You may be asking yourself, "Shouldn't something be said about those electronic charge card printers? Don't they keep you from doing this?" I have two comments about them.

First, now and again they separate and store representatives need to depend on the old manual strategy. Thus, to utilize transcribed receipts once in for some time, that would be your excuse.

Second, running calculator tape through the printer of a PC can create in a real sense many sorts and styles of true looking receipts, complete with logos assuming you like. Simply duplicate the organizations of some you've really seen.

Indeed, there are various tiny printers accessible for PCs planned explicitly for names and receipts. They are modest. You can get one with the product to run it for under $150 new. Assuming you purchase somebody's pre-owned one, you'll spend under $50.

Your PC can be the best falsifier of reports you might at any point request. Circles of clasp workmanship are accessible for every one of the large companies around the country. Their logos are on them. Numerous more modest town inns actually print their receipts on regular clear paper. The expense of a printer for your PC is under $100.

If you need genuine clear solicitations from lodgings, you can get some in at least

three different ways. The first is request it. Tell the representative, "I simply love the arrangement of your receipts. I'm certain my supervisors might want to check whether it would work for our organization. Would I be able to have a couple of clear sheets to show them?"

Often, stacking their printers or a side-effect of creating solicitations the entire day, many clear pages result and are kept by the agents for use as scratch paper. Assuming you see clear solicitations lying around, act somewhat bothered and inquire, "I want a piece of scratch paper, would I be able to have one of those clear solicitations there?"

Obviously, there is the old backup of examining the waste basket. Typically, the late shift wipes out the bins for the day shift and places the sacks of garbage out for the morning janitor to get. They are regularly in simple reach and sometimes watched.

More insights regarding receipts later.

Your Company's Rules to Watch

Some organizations have been composing new cost approaches to close a significant number of the provisos and keep their workers from undermining their cost reports. As a rule, their demonstration of shutting one opening opens another significantly bigger opening. In any case, the initial phase in cushioning your costs and pulling off it, is to see all of the rules.

Per Diems

From the Latin for "each day", this is a sweeping fixed dollar sum intended to cover every one of your costs. Organizations don't expect you to turn in a receipt for these. Truth be told the entire thought behind an organization utilizing per diems for costs is to decrease desk work and lower the time spent by managers inspecting cost reports
- exactly what we need.

If the representative spends more than the outlay, it is their misfortune. In the event that the worker spends less, they get to keep the distinction, apparently to cover overages on different days. The less cash you spend, the more cash you keep. On the off chance that there at any point was an opportunity to be modest, this is it.

The IRS has set up guidelines for the sums paid, in light of region of the country in which you are voyaging and sort of routine set of expenses your organization pays. Most organizations guarantee they are paying the IRS endorsed sum, yet most don't, or they decide to pay the least, paying little mind to the area in which you are voyaging. Go to the library and turn upward the rules.

If you observe they are not paying the right sum, challenge your organization to refresh their outlay adds up to be in "consistence" with the IRS. Assuming they won't, you might have the option to recover the distinction on your

individual pay tax.

Simple per diems start with accidental costs. An organization might pay all movement, housing, and suppers for a representative and afterward offer them a little charge ($10) each day to cover any remaining costs like clothing and tips while on site.

The most muddled per diems are intended to cover all movement, housing, and feast expenses and can be very enormous. You see these for the most part in the business field and specifically with what are classified "free" agents. At times and regions, this could be many dollars per day.

The most ordinarily utilized outlay is intended to cover suppers and odds and ends. The organization pays genuine costs like airfare, inns, and rental vehicles, and afterward anticipates that the employee should deal with the outlay to cover all the other things. This kind of outlay, as per IRS rules, changes concerning the piece of the nation voyaged, yet goes somewhere in the range of $25 and $50.

If you have the more confounded, comprehensive routine set of expenses, you're as of now likely a sufficient skin-stone that you realize the amount you can streamline to make additional bucks, so I'll restrict my remarks to the less difficult, more normal one for suppers and miscellaneous items.

Streamlining is the way to stashing however much of the outlay as could be expected. Pick an inn which serves a free breakfast. Take two or three bits of natural product with you to eat during the day, and you can in all probability skip lunch. A few inns likewise have evening "glad hours" with free appetizers, which frequently are enough for a meal.

If you need to eat for as little as possible, attempt the amazing openings of supermarkets or home improvement shops. They frequently have quarter dollar franks and free beverages. Observe the eateries with everything you can eat buffets. Snacks here are two or three bucks less expensive than supper for similar things. Eating a major, later lunch could permit you to skip dinner.

Obviously, any time anybody needs to get you lunch or supper, let them. Regardless of whether they're a salesman. Better to have a free supper and pay attention to an attempt to seal the deal you would rather not hear, than to pay for your own dinner out of your per diem.

Stay at lodgings which havc a small scale or full kitchen and fix your own meals.

They are less expensive and regularly better 100% of the time than eateries. Simply having a fridge in your room can save you enormous dollars on your per diem.

Never ask a bellperson to convey your sack assuming your are solid enough.

Don't tip them except if they truly did you an assistance, especially if you wanted

to convey your own pack however they demanded to do it without anyone's help. Better to be reprimanded by the ringer representative than to discard great cash. Really take a look at your stuff inside the air terminal. Try not to pay the sky cap to do how the carriers will help free.

If stopping, while out and about, is important for your routine set of expenses, discover some free stopping as opposed to utilizing the lodging's carport. Better to walk a square or thereabouts, then, at that point, to lose a couple of bucks a day.

If stopping, back home at the air terminal, would be important for your outlay, ask companions or your mate to drive you to the air terminal and get you. On the off chance that you have none, verify whether a taxi ride to and fro to the air terminal is less expensive than the rate you'd pay at the stopping garages.

Charge Card Receipts vs. Tear Off Tabs

In circumstances where the cost strategy pays for individual suppers, a few organizations have attempted to forestall entries of the normal remove eatery receipt, by expecting you to turn in the genuine charge card slip. I've as of now talked about several different ways around this.

The organization strategy commonly peruses something like, "... representatives should eat at properties which acknowledge Mastercards and will utilize the Visa in all circumstances, except if the property acknowledges nothing however cash."

If all worker submitted receipts were straightforward, this would be an inept approach, as legitimately a burger joint or other inexpensive food place which works on money would be less expensive than practically each of the spots which acknowledge charge cards. The organization would wind up paying more than they had to.

It's ideal to push the envelope on this one. Assuming you are skipping lunch and turning in the detach receipts for a couple of bucks, I'd do it until somebody questions it.

Then you may say, "Hmm, I know the approach, yet the least expensive spots I can find to eat which assume praise cards would've cost me somewhere around ten bucks for lunch. This burger joint was just four and a half. Do you truly need me to spend two times as a significant part of the organization's cash for lunch than I have to?"

If your chief or the organization answers that you should utilize the charge card, they've quite recently given you unlimited authority to swindle. Presently you can turn in higher dollar, fake Mastercard receipts. Additionally, assuming you report the discussion, you have what adds up to a "escape prison free" card.

If at some later date, they question your costs, you can highlight your documentation and say, "I needed to set aside you parents cash, however no, you advised me to spend two times however much I needed to. I'm confounded. Am I truly assumed to

hold down costs or blow superfluous cash to agree with the policy?"

If your organization acknowledges the detach receipt for eateries, then, at that point, you are good to go. Assuming that they require the charge slip, you'll simply need to get more creative.

Airline Tickets

I will cover carrier tickets exhaustively later in the book. The carrier is a decent method for adding large dollars to your cost report and get it into your pockets. To do it, you really want to discover what is required when you present your report.

The best developments for undermining costs were E-tickets, which don't have the commonplace receipt. The worker gets an agenda and a receipt duplicate. There is no genuine ticket. You appear at the air terminal at what you trust is the legitimate overall setting. They take your name and print you a loading up pass.

The E-ticket made an exceptionally simple technique to cushion cost reports. Verify whether your boss requirements the receipt duplicate, schedule, or the pre-owned tickets. I'll explain to you why this is significant later in the book.

If your organization's travel planner actually gives genuine tickets, you again should see whether they pay from the receipt which is regularly the last page in the bundle, from the schedule, or from the pre-owned loading up pass.

It likewise has an effect in a calculated manner, with regards to whether they charge your own Mastercard, or the organization's accounts.

Hotels and Rental Cars

Again, a few organizations expect you to present the real charge card receipt. Some compensation from a receipt or folio printed by a lodging or rental organization. It's vital to know which one the organization needs for payment.

Later in the book, we'll take a gander at the distinction it makes for lodgings, yet regardless, on the off chance that you invest a little energy and pre-arranging, inns can be a rewarding method for cushioning your cost reports in practically untraceable ways.

Also later in the book, we'll check out rental vehicle techniques. They are the hardest ones to cushion straightforwardly. In a roundabout way, they are a decent wellspring of a couple of bucks to a great extent for stopping and fuel. To have the option to trade out for greater dollars with rental vehicle offices, you should realize which receipt is satisfactory by your company.

Taxi Cabs & Limousines

You can cushion a huge load of cash around here, every last bit of it relying on what

documentation your organization will accept.

Don't let the term limousine fool you. In numerous urban communities this is a major revolting van, packed with however many individuals as a shoe horn will allow. In different urban areas, one outstandingly Indianapolis, the genuine limousine administrations keep their vehicles occupied with during the day doing air terminal runs. In Indy, they are frequently less expensive than customary cabs and there is a sure measure of self image stroking which accompanies moving out of a stretch limo at a hotel.

Either way, in most all urban communities taxi receipts are really the backs of business cards, and generally inexpensively and roughly printed business cards. If inexplicably you can't get a couple "extra" receipts from a cabbie, you could unquestionably print them yourself.

Some organizations will acknowledge these as verification, thus you can clearly fill in whatever sums you need. Different organizations will possibly acknowledge them in the event that they are filled in and endorsed by the cabbie. For a couple of additional bucks on the tip, cabbies will fill in whatever number you ask.

If you don't must have a marked and filled in receipt from the cabbie, a couple of additional bucks on the tip will get you a small bunch of clear receipts. Cabbies are valid business visionaries. A couple of bucks cash for a couple of bits of paper, is a decent arrangement for them as well.

Unfortunately, a few bosses expect you to utilize a charge card for these taxi trips. The cabbies disdain them, since they need to do unique techniques to deal with the card and their tips as covered the card are accounted for to the IRS. It is difficult to find support from any cabbie on charge cards.

Just be certain you know or have tried which sorts of receipts your organization will accept.

General Comments

There is a distinction between what the cost arrangement says and what really happens when bills are paid. The main way you know, is to test the system.

Remember I let you know your supervisor truly doesn't want to invest a great deal of energy perusing your reports, and their secretary is even more averse to care.

Generally, in the event that everything is upheld with some sort of receipt and if everything sums accurately, your manager will sign it.

The records payable office pays hundreds or even a huge number of bills regular. They have even less motivating force to "review" your cost report. They will as a rule review to check whether everything aggregates and foots, and if your supervisor marked it. Assuming it looks right and is endorsed by your chief, they pay it.

Your chief and the records payable individuals don't dependably know the documentation strategy very well either, so try things out. A tad at an at once, or two detach receipts rather than the charge slips the approach requires. Assuming that they traverse, attempt some more. The greater amount and recurrence of receipts you get by them, the better track history you have for covering any future discoveries.

Let's say one day your manager is being meddling and tracks down a detach receipt.

When they advise you that arrangement requires something different, you just answer, "Indeed, I've been handing those over throughout recent months. You've said nothing and A/P has been paying them. I just idea it was okay."

In many cases, the manager will assent. The last thing they need to concede to A/P is that they have been allowing inappropriate receipts to squeeze by. The manager will generally say, "Indeed, assuming A/P is paying them, it should be alright. I'm not going to over-lead them."

Even assuming everybody says to quit submitting them, you can apologize and vow to not repeat the experience. You actually figured out how to get all of the others through and paid. Then you can wait another couple of months and start running one or two through again until someone else notices.

The main rule of cushioning your costs, is similar first rule as paying less expenses to the IRS. It is: "In the event that you volunteer to adhere to the guidelines, you'll get nothing. Assuming they at any point need it back, they'll request it."

Chapter Two

Legitimate Perks To Remember

There are a few worthwhile advantages which come to you as a side advantage of having a business ledger. Before I go into the deceptive ways of acquiring benefits from your costs, I needed to examine with you an assortment of ways of expanding your advantages from those strategies which are legal.

Even around here, there are organizations out there who are attempting to sort out some method for taking all your extra focuses and aircraft mileage away from you and put them into their pockets. Would an organization be able to profit from your aircraft miles and such? Definitely they can! Would the chiefs in the organization be able to profit from your aircraft miles? Absolutely!

If you recall prior in the book, I let you know the leaders will turn on you instantly on the off chance that they can help their own positions. This is a confirmation.

The organization gets restricted advantages from this strategy, yet the leaders can straightforwardly profit from the free tickets, benefit sharing from reduced

costs, and moves up to initially class accommodations.

Indeed, in the event that your organization books a major show, they will explicitly obstruct the singular flyers from utilizing their own regular customer numbers. They will hit an arrangement with an aircraft to unite the trips as a trade-off for various free tickets.

I've organized shows for the organization and I can say in those cases, the free tickets were not utilized for participants. That multitude of free tickets were given to the leader of the organization, for use on future "business" trips. Assuming the genuine intention was to set aside the organization cash, for what reason weren't the free tickets utilized for a portion of the show goers?

The public authority, by means of the IRS, has even attempted to sort out some method for making you pay charges on your regular customer focuses and other programs.

Besides it being hard to quantify and esteem, the court difficulties to this will require many years, as it straightforwardly impacts individual sacred privileges of the public.

Let's investigate every one of the significant classes accessible to you. I'll disclose a few methods for augmenting your advantages and caution you of ways your organization will attempt to keep you from getting those perks.

Airlines

Every significant carrier has a long standing customer program. Despite the fact that they change in how miles are incorporated, followed, and gave for flights, they all observe a few comparative guidelines. Their principles must be comparative. On the off chance that one aircraft offered a fundamentally unique and better program, the rest would need to take action accordingly or hazard having each of their individuals bounce ship.

Legally, the carriers deny any plot around here. They need to in light of the fact that it would disregard hostile to trust laws. That is the thing that they guarantee, yet two or three years prior, one of the transporters raised the miles important to get free flights and brought down the base flight miles paid per portion. In no time, each in turn, every one of the aircrafts changed their program rules. This is all in all a coincidence.

Just in the event that you don't have a clue, this is the manner by which these regular customer programs work. You join into a program. This quite often is at no charge. Each time you fly, you or your travel planner enters your record number on your ticket and you are credited naturally for the miles you fly.

Most projects provide you with at least 500 miles for fragments you fly which are not exactly that numerous miles. For a flight longer than 500 miles, they credit to your record the genuine miles flown.

An intriguing exemption for keep an eye out for, is this. Suppose you are on a flight which leaves Las Vegas for Memphis. Your plane stops in Houston, however you don't change planes. The aircrafts call this a continuation flight.

The carrier will pay you the straight line distance from Las Vegas to Memphis, not the complete miles of the two sections. Assuming you do the math on this one, you'll see this can be a considerable loss of miles.

The aircrafts further incent you to consume your flying dollars, by setting "levels" in the program, at which you begin to improve benefits. How about we make an imaginary aircraft called Princess Air.

In the mileage program for Princess Air, we credit you a point for each mile you fly up to 25,000 miles per year. By then, we send you another ID card and illuminate you that you are presently an individual from the Silver Club. As a silver flyer, you acquire 1.5 focuses per mile, your own booking number to call, and the capacity to buy minimal expense moves up to First Class, which you can save 24 hours in front of time.

Once you fly 50,000 miles in a year, we knock you to Gold Club. As a

Gold Club part, you procure twofold focuses per mile flown, we send you a few free update coupons a couple of times each year, we permit you to book First Class redesigns 72 hours early, and you get free beverages on the flight.

Once you fly 100,000 miles, you accomplish Platinum Status. As a Platinum flyer, we give you triple miles, free stopping at the air terminal, and your very own airline steward on-board.

Okay, In this way I went excessively far, however the carriers will truly add rewards for you as you construct an ever increasing number of miles with them. So, assuming you need the greatest advantages from an aircraft program, you really want to fly one transporter however much you can. This is the place where your boss starts to cause you grief.

Your organization will need you to fly the most reduced toll paying little mind to the transporter. (Would you be shocked to know, that top chiefs are normally absolved from this approach?) You can secure yourself a little by pursuing EVERYONE's program. That way, regardless of who they request that you fly, you'll get some credit.

Another method for ensuring your focuses, is to offer flying Saturday evenings to lessen the airfare. Your manager will adore you. Flights Monday through Friday are substantially more costly. They are regularly $500 more costly. At these greater costs, the probability of there being a less expensive passage on one more aircraft than your essential decision is higher. Assuming you fly a carrier that actually offers even lower tolls with a Saturday night stay, fly them.

Remember, Saturday night stays end at 12 PM at your beginning air terminal. On west coast to east drift flights, you can take a "red eye" flight leaving at 11:30 pm and show up before the expected time Sunday morning. Your manager prefers the diminished charge, and you can get a free day of touring in the town you are visiting. Assuming you can figure out how to rest on the flight, it is an incredible deal.

Another method for trying not to need to fly a substitute transporter, is to fly a confounded course. All in all, you would track down a great deal of value rivalry on departures from Chicago to Los Angeles. You will not find too many discount bidding wars for a flight that goes from New York to Detroit for a couple of days, then to Denver for a day, and then back to New York. Regularly on these more muddled routings, it is less expensive 100% of the time to have you fly on one carrrier for the whole trip.

On certain carriers, there are covered up advantages which they don't promote. On certain transporters, when you arrive at a specific mileage level, ordinarily around 50,000 miles, you start the following year at your old reward level and don't need to begin once again. This implies as much as an additional 50,000 miles the following year in reward points.

On certain transporters, the more significant level individuals can knock lower positioning flyers for overhauls, backup flights, and even flight reservations. On the genuine trip in mentor class, the higher positioned flyers get to barricade first and sit front, nearer to the entryway, and the middle seats are hindered as late as possible to boost the possibilities you will be sitting two in a three man path. Fundamentally, the carriers do numerous things to compensate the individuals who construct miles with them.

Airlines permit you to hand your miles over for an assortment of things. You can get free passes to basically anyplace on the planet. Prime destinations such as Hawaii and Europe take a premium number of points. On certain transporters, assuming you need to fly from New York to Hawaii, you need to utilize focuses to purchase a mainland United States ticket and afterward purchase one more ticket for the mainland United States to Hawaii, so be careful.

Besides tickets, a few transporters permit you to involve your focuses for updates for you and some other individual flying with you. Some permit you to involve focuses to purchase enrollments in their carrier clubs, where you improve admittance to telephones, free bites, TVs, and more satisfying surroundings.

From time to time, the aircrafts will hold barters where you can offer focuses for intriguing excursions and get-aways. These can be incredible deals.

Moreover, when you recover miles for tickets, you will as a rule get different coupons for overhauls or free days with the aircraft's rental vehicle and hotel

partners.

Some businesses in all actuality do have a cost approach which would permit you to involve your preferred customer credits for business travel and afterward the organization pays you for the ticket. This arrangement appears to be really great for you, as you get cash with the expectation of complimentary miles. You must be cautious however, as they only from time to time repay you the maximum the ticket is really worth.

The business typically pays a rate (half or 75%) of the most reduced toll accessible. You should adjust the cash you get from assisting the organization with what a free ticket on an individual excursion may be worth to you. Later in the book, I'll show you one more method for transforming those miles into cash - at top dollar!

Airline preferred customer credits are probably the best advantage a voyaging money manager can use. You really want to give a valiant effort to shield those miles from being lost by or to your boss. You additionally need to do the best to expand your reward points.

One of the most effective ways to "parlay" your focuses with the carriers is to connect it to inn programs, rental vehicle projects, and charge cards.

Airline Sponsored Charge Cards

Every significant aircraft has a Mastercard partner, it's ordinarily with one enormous bank, which pays you miles for your charges as a whole. On the off chance that you are the sort of individual who takes care of their Mastercard adjusts each month, they are an extraordinary wellspring of extra miles with the carriers. Assuming you ordinarily convey an equilibrium on your cards, the arrangement isn't excessively great, as these cards generally have a lot higher rate charge than you can get with other bank cards.

By getting one of these cards, each dollar you charge for tickets, vehicle rentals, inns, suppers, and even your new pair of sneakers, acquires you miles with the aircraft. Commonly the rate is one mile for each dollar. A few premium cards like Diner's Club will pay products of two or four miles for each dollar.

Some of these cards have yearly charges which will be deferred or decreased by the organization assuming that you are a higher positioning long standing customer. A portion of these program cards have yearly cutoff points to the miles you can accumulate, except if you achieve the higher program status. In any case, the more you utilize the card, the more miles you collect.

The most concerning issue with these cards is your manager not permitting you to involve the card for movement related issues. For what reason would they do that? Cash to them, of course!

Often a business will make "accessible" to their representatives a "corporate card" from one of the majors like American Express or Diner's Club. It put corporate in enclosures, as the main thing the company does is put their name on the card with you. The partnership doesn't ensure the card in any capacity at all.

There are valid corporate cards, where an organization takes care of the bills straightforwardly, yet just the top leaders will get one. (Perceive how it keeps on contrasting?) The equilibrium of the representatives will get the other "corporate card" for use in their travels.

The organization works an arrangement with say Diner's Club, where Diner's Club consents to postpone their enrollment charge for people.

Consequently, the organization consents to compose an arrangement which powers representatives to solely utilize that card while voyaging. This guarantees the accuse card provider of as much volume as possible.

You are still by and by answerable for the charges as a whole and paying the month to month explanations. On the off chance that your own credit is terrible, you will most likely be unable to fit the bill for the card. Assuming you default on an installment, it will be your own credit which is impacted, not the employer.

What's in it for me? Very little. On the off chance that you pay an extra charge, you may get a portion of the extra miles credited to your record, yet Anywayme card organizations won't give mileage credit to significant aircrafts like United or American. So, assuming you're content with miles for flyiing optional transporters, it's okay.

What's in it for my organization? A great deal. Mastercard organizations charge an expense to the carriers, lodgings, and such of somewhere in the range of 2 and 4 percent on all charges to the card. More volume implies more pay to the charge card organization. In most corporate projects, your manager gets a discount from the card organization. They pretty much "split" the charges. For an organization with ten million dollars in movement, a one percent refund is still $100,000.

Everything thing you can manage, assuming that your manager has one of these approach programs, is to in any case attempt to utilize your own carrier Visa however much as could reasonably be expected. The arrangement for the most part says you should utilize the corporate card or hazard the organization declining to pay the expense.

Nice danger, however I might want to see the compassion a business would get in court assuming that a worker needed to eat an enormous cost and afterward needed to sue the business to get it paid. Generally, the approach danger is utilized like the IRS utilizes the danger of a review. The odds of it really happening is slim,

however at that point its simple danger happening is to the point of keeping a great many people legit and following the rules.

Your smartest choice, is to utilize a corporate card any place you have no choice,

i.e. with the company mandated travel agent, and use your own card everywhere else until they tell you to stop. The corporate card will most likely be American Express or Diner's Club. Like the television commercials state, there are still a lot of places which accept Mastercard and Visa, which is more than likely what your airline card is anyway; but they do not accept American Express.

A mostly secret program through some significant Mastercard organizations is an eatery refund program. These typically cost you a yearly expense of $25 or so to join, however assuming that you do a decent measure of business amusement, the advantages to you could add up quickly.

In these projects, your charges at "part" eateries is tracked. When you join, they provide you with a rundown of cafés all around the world which have a place with the program. Toward the month's end, whatever you've spent at these chosen eateries will be added up to, and you will get a check for as much as 20% of the absolute bill.

This is an incredible arrangement in the event that you can pull it off. You get aircraft mile credit and 20% money refunded to you, for the costs paid 100 percent by your employer.

Hotel Point Programs

Many of the significant chains like Hilton, Hyatt, Marriott, and Holiday Inn, have connect projects to the carriers. In these projects, in the event that you show up in a city on say an American Airlines flight, you can give them your carrier account number and they will acknowledge you for 500 or 1000 miles.

Keep your eyes and ears open, as at times they run advancements where you get twofold or triple miles for a specific number of night stays, or by remaining in a particular lodging in a city.

The inns only sometimes request a ticket or ticket as confirmation, so regardless of whether you drove your vehicle or flew in on an alternate aircraft, show your aircraft enrollment card and request credit. More often than not, you'll get it.

Aside from these immediate connection kinds of projects, large numbers of the chains run their own point programs. These come in a few structures with differing benefits, yet in the event that your organization permits you to pick your inn inside specific dollar rules, conforming to a specific lodging network can procure pretty enormous benefits.

Some inns give you a point or two for each dollar you spend. These focuses can then be utilized to "purchase" items or administrations from a list they distribute. These items can go from an extravagant windshield ice scrubber to enormous screen TVs and even around-theworld trips.

Some inns permit you to recover your focuses with the expectation of complimentary evenings of stay or moves up to better rooms. These can be exceptionally valuable to you in arranging get-aways on your off time.

Some inns have programs where they don't count the dollars, however offer you a free night's visit following ten or twelve evenings in their chain.

These night stays don't need to be at one area nor on sequential evenings. You can gather these all around the country, the entire year. A few chains even give you the adaptability to change over these into aircraft miles as opposed to taking their coupon for a free night's stay.

Notwithstanding these immediate advantages, many chains permit you to assemble focuses and accomplish club levels like the carriers do. Your "gold" status might procure you a free breakfast and a paper that the normal individual doesn't get. Your "platinum" status might overhaul you to suites at standard room rates when available.

The manner in which focuses compound on excursions for work will be talked about later, yet getting aircraft mileage focuses from the inn for your visit, paid for with the charge card which pays you aircraft miles, helps fabricate focuses quickly.

Rental Car Point Programs

Generally, the rental vehicle organizations will restrict themselves to the connection sort of program where they will credit your aircraft mileage account with 500 or 1000 miles if show up on that carrier's flight.

The significant rental vehicle organizations take an interest in practically every carrier's program, so odds are you will actually want to get credit with whatever transporter you flew. Assuming you need credit with a particular transporter, you should attempt exactly the same thing you would with a hotel.

The rental vehicle counter agents only sometimes request to see the ticket stub, so have convenient a flight number from your carrier of decision (accessible by perusing screens in the air terminal) which showed up at an at once, and give it to the representative. Request credit. You will in all likelihood get it.

Something else to remember with the vehicle rental organizations, is your organization's "public" contract, assuming they have one. These generally permit you to lease an assortment of vehicle sizes with rates which shift by just a dollar or two every day from the least expensive rate.

This is convenient for two reasons. In the first place, some of the time the rental organization will

pay premium focuses, twofold or triple, on the off chance that you lease a particular class of vehicle. Ask, either when holding or getting the vehicle, assuming they are running any "administrator specials" at this location.

The subsequent explanation is basically solace for you. Normally there are two kinds of administrative work on a vehicle rental - the agreement and the receipt. The agreement is the desk work you regularly convey with you as you drive the vehicle. You get your receipt, normally a PC print out and charge slip receipt, when you return the car.

The agreement shows the class of vehicle you leased in some code structure, number or letter. The solicitations barely at any point show the sort of vehicle leased. Rental vehicle rates differ radically around the nation, so except if your manager sees the agreement, they have no clue about whether you leased a $50 per day, sub-minimized GEO Metro in New York or a $40 per day, elite execution Mustang in Indianapolis.

By knowing the kind of receipts adequate for accommodation on your cost report, you could lease a superior vehicle, get extra focuses, and partake in easy street. Ponder it.

Parlaying Points for Maximum Benefit

Assuming you have the opportunity to single out, who you fly and where you stay, we should perceive how you can function a work excursion to expand your focuses and aircraft miles. Suppose that you have a place with a carrier long standing customer plan and you've booked an adequate number of miles that you've made the club level which pays you twofold miles.

You should require a multi day excursion for work from New York to the Los Angeles region. The genuine office you are visiting is somewhere between LAX and Orange County air terminals. The airfare is something very similar to LAX or Orange County,
$1500 round trip.

You do some checking, by calling distinctive rental organizations on their 800 numbers, and discover a rental organization is running an advancement at the Orange County air terminal on Mustang convertibles. You get the moderate size vehicle pace of $40 every day in addition to significantly increase aircraft miles.

You in all actuality do some seriously looking at and see that a significant lodging close to the air terminal is paying twofold miles and twofold inn program points.

You pay for the excursion on your carrier charge card, which acquires you aircraft miles. During your excursion, you should have two meals for ten individuals each. On this outing, you could wind up with Visa charges which complete something like this:

Airline tickets $1500
Rental Car ($40 x 4 days + charges) $
200 Hotel ($80 x 4 days + charges) $
400
Two Hosted Dinners (10 individuals x $30)
$ 600 Meals and odds and ends $ 100
Total charges $2800

When you total up your preferred customer credits for this excursion you could have aggregates like this:

Airline Mileage (2500 miles every way)

5000 Airline Bonus for Club Status 5000

Charge Card Point Mileage 2800

Rental Mileage (500 x triple) 1500

Hotel Mileage (500 x twofold) 1000

Total Miles 15,300

So, on one work excursion, you've acquired than 15,000 miles on your aircraft mileage account. In many projects, free tickets are 25,000 miles, so you are over 60% toward getting a free trip.

What's more, on the off chance that you held every one of your suppers at the eatery which is important for your charge card organization's discount program, they will send you a check for 20% or $120 for the dinners. You additionally will get any of the advantages your inn program focuses will buy.

All of these are benefits cost you only a little arranging time, and were thoughtfully paid for by your employer.

Additional Benefits to Consider

Before I leave this section for the greener grounds of cushioning your cost report, I thought I'd help you to remember what a definitive advantage of having a business ledger can mean - FREE excursions to colorful places.

Collecting these focuses and coupons throughout the year, take care of huge when time off comes around. Free miles for flights, free inn evenings in redesigned hotels, free vehicle rentals, and limits to attractions are only the beginning.

Just this year, I went on an outing to Hawaii for seven days. Utilizing carrier miles, my mate and I flew with every available amenity the nation over and afterward to Hawaii. Complete worth of the tickets assuming I had been compelled to buy them, $9000.

Using a few aircraft miles, in addition to inn focuses, we remained in a beach front suite at a Hyatt resort. Absolute worth of the room assuming that I had paid for it, $2625.

I utilized a few vehicle rental coupons to lease a lively convertible. Absolute worth assuming that I

had paid for it, $275.

I involved coupons and associations for limited suppers, a day journey, and a helicopter ride. The complete expense decrease of these added up to about $300.

To spare the gritty details, by being shrewd the entire year, watching where I remained and counting each aircraft mile I could get, I got a for all intents and purposes free, weeklong excursion in heaven worth more than $12,000.

Since you didn't pay for this with your own hardearned cash, the get-away is a pre-charge raise of more than $20,000.

I rest my case!

Chapter Three

How to Make Money on Airlines

If you will bring in enormous cash in cushioning your cost report, it's a good idea in any case the biggest dollar things accessible. Carrier tickets are one of the greatest travel costs, so we'll start there.

Most individuals see aircraft tickets and can't help thinking about how they might actually get cash back on cost reports. The main component in bringing in cash is the means by which intently your manager tracks your travels.

For the vast majority of us, when we're out of the workplace in the field, nobody calls or determines the status of us. They as a rule utilize the voice message for correspondence and the odds of somebody really calling the branch office that we're visiting is slim.

Indeed, in several positions I've held, sticking around the workplace, regardless of how useful you were, raised the doubts of the managers. They'd inquire, "How does that individual respond?" On the other hand, assuming I was "in the field", they thought I was truly on top of things.

I could in a real sense let them know I was traveling to the Reno office for a few days and hang out in the club. However long they didn't call the workplace and I checked my phone message, I got back to a typical office who accepted I was buckling down. Assuming that they did call the workplace, I could simply guarantee I became sick and just neglected to tell the branch.

How would you bring in cash on your costs when the carriers control the tickets? A great deal of it relies on the sorts of receipts your organization expects you to use in support up your expenses.

What you can pull off, likewise relies upon who books your flight. You can do a lot more things assuming you can utilize your own travel planner or then again on the off chance that you can book tickets on your PC. Assuming that you are secured in a travel planner inside your office, you are somewhat restricted, however not shutout.

Another variable in what you can pull off, is the thing that sort of tagging you get. The E-ticket, where you don't really get a ticket, yet appear at a carrier counter to check in for your flight utilizing your name, are awesome. E-tickets open ways of ripping off your manager in manners we never had and they never thought existed.

The E-ticket was imagined via carriers to diminish their expenses. They guarantee it is advantageous to you as a flyer, yet nobody has had the option to disclose it to me such that appears to be legit. Various individuals have attempted, however the straightforward truth is it saves the carriers cost and they need to do it. Assuming they generally get together and constrain us to utilize them, what can we do?

Your travel planner loves them, as they never need to convey the genuine passes to you. They can either email or fax you a duplicate of the timetable. This saves them huge load of cash in postage and expedited delivery charges.

I might want to initially begin by characterizing a few things which I should discuss later.

Itinerary - An agenda is a piece of paper which records timetable of movement, affirmation numbers, phone numbers, and some other relevant travel information.

Receipt - There are two kinds of receipts. There is the receipt you get from the travel planner which is most frequently called your E-ticket, and afterward there might be a different charge card receipt.

Invoice - When utilizing E-tickets, your receipt may really be called a receipt copy.

Boarding Pass - When you check in for your flight, they will regularly print you a ticket, which is the thing that the old "genuine ticket" resembled, and it has your real seat task for the flight.

Some businesses pay from the real E-ticket or receipt, while a few managers need those in addition to your agenda. You want to sort out the ones your boss needs. The reasons will turn out to be clear a tad later.

It is likewise essential for you to comprehend an unexpected surprise about aircraft ticket estimating plans. There's a boundless assortment of ticket choices and rules administering your tickets which can affect you and your capacity to bring in cash on your expenses.

Unrestricted Fares - Most business travel happens on what is known as a full passage or unhindered admission ticket premise. Most business travel is Monday through Friday and regularly reserved without a second to spare, so they can't exploit markdown tolls. Insights have shown that under half of the flyers today are business flyers, yet they produce 80% of the incomes for carriers, since they are paying for pricey tickets. These tickets are absolutely refundable and absolutely changeable.

Restricted Fares - These tickets cost somewhat less, and have a few limitations regarding when you can make changes, what those progressions cost, and regardless of whether they can be discounted or credited to one more ticket.

Discount Fares - It used to be assuming you could remain over on a Saturday night and purchase your tickets seven, fourteen, or 21 days ahead of time, you could get an extremely modest ticket. Presently it alludes to the least expensive ticket you can purchase. Generally the tickets have numerous limitations. They can not be changed without paying an expense and they can not be discounted. Much of the time, without breaking the bank, they can be credited toward one more ticket inside a year.

Back-to-back Booking - this used to be a way that assuming you need to book without a second to spare, you could in any case figure out how to get a rebate ticket. A full admission ticket from Chicago to Los Angeles might cost $1400 full circle. But if you were tricky, you can buy two discount tickets which total less than the full fare. You do this booking your outbound departure from Chicago and a return fourteen days later; and afterward book the other ticket to go full circle beginning from Los Angeles on your right return date and a return fourteen days later. You discarded the unused back equal parts of every one of those tickets they actually absolute not exactly full passage. (On the off chance that you were great, you could get your boss to pay for these two tickets and timetable different parts to give you a free week-end full circle on another date. Play with the dates to see what I'm saying.)

Other than these overall depictions, it is almost difficult to comprehend aircraft evaluating. A while ago when Denver opened their new air terminal, the city of Colorado Springs was running advancements to urge individuals to utilize their air terminal. A ticket to go full circle from Denver to Los Angeles, was $400 more costly than tickets what began and finished in Colorado Springs, yet were associated through Denver. Does additional trips for less cash make sense?

Changing Discount Tickets

The aircrafts authoritatively let you know that these tickets are non-variable and non-refundable, yet there are things you can do. You can drop your booking on a limited ticket and the ticket will "pend" inside most carrier PCs for a year. You can then credit them toward another ticket, for a charge. The costs run somewhere in the range of $35 and $60 per change, contingent on the aircraft.

Exactly the same thing should be possible to secure mileage focuses due to terminate. In the event that you have a few record miles due to lapse, you book a free outing pass to any place and at whatever point. Following a couple of days, call them and drop the booking. By and large, those tickets will remain dynamic for an extra year without a charge.

With a portion of the fresher regular customer account programs, the transporter will re-credit your record for the places. A few transporters' PCs can acknowledge the record for the first termination dates, so they'd in any case pass on. Assuming that is your transporter, you might attempt this stunt. For most projects, you really want to recover the tickets by termination dates, however they can be utilized on tickets as much as a year from that day.

Accepting Overbooked Offers

Airlines will regularly overbook flights, wagering that a specific level of individuals will drop or change their flight, hence opening up the required seats. Carriers track this cautiously over the long haul on exceptionally famous courses. They really are very great "bookies" with regards to this.

Every sometimes, they commit errors and the overbooking brings about an excessive number of individuals attempting to get on a similar flight. The airline will then make an announcement over the loudspeaker, asking for some volunteers to give up their seat in return for some money, coupons, or meals, plus a seat on a later flight.

If you are adaptable in your timetable and you can chip in, this can turn out great for you. Likewise with all circumstances, there are a couple of things you want to know. The aircraft needs to spend as little as conceivable to get you to surrender your seat.

This first thing you and every one of the other potential volunteers need to know, is this is actually a bartering. The carrier needs to get chips in or deny somebody getting on the plane, so you have a considerable amount of leverage.

The starting bid from the aircraft will for the most part be something like a $100 rebate coupon for use on future aircraft tickets, in addition to a ticket on the following flight that is going to your objective. Assuming that nobody chomps at this level, the carrier will up the proposition. I have seen the aircraft offer a top notch ticket on a later flight, in addition to two tickets with the expectation of complimentary travel anyplace in the United States, and supper coupons while hanging tight for your flight.

If the carrier has a later flight, and it is likewise overbooked, they may offer you a ticket on another transporter. In the event that you need the mileage credit, you are in an ideal situation sitting tight for a later trip on a similar transporter. On the off chance that you acknowledge the flight on another aircraft and they are not your transporter of decision, you won't get mileage kudos for the flight. Your credit will be on the flight they shift you to, assuming you have a long standing customer number with them.

The aircrafts can and will offer various things. They have a few sorts of coupons giving limits on future flights. A few coupons restrict you to 10% of the ticket value you are purchasing and some are very much like money without limits.

The aircraft can offer you free flight coupons for movement anyplace in the United States, great for a little while. They can likewise offer you suppers at the air terminal, or even off-site eateries. Assuming that your deferral expects you to remain for the time being, they will give a lodging and recompenses to dinners, and even toiletry packs, assuming you request them.

When getting the later flight, you ought to consistently request a move up to initially class. Assuming they have the room, it costs them nothing, so more often than not you can get it. Ask pleasantly and genuinely. Airline stewards and door laborers disdain pushy and upsetting individuals, and have magnificent methods of settling the score with them. To wind up in the last column, back in the corner close to an uproarious motor, situated between two shouting kids, be great when asking.

Making Money With Discount Coupons

There are numerous ways for you to gain rebate coupons for aircraft travel. Banks offer them when you open new records. The carriers will send them to you in some cases as a component of your regular customer status changes. Rental vehicle organizations and lodgings will give them to you for utilizing them.

The fact is, aircrafts love them, as the vast majority of the coupons are restricted to say $25 on a trip of $300 or more. The carrier actually got $275 or more for the ticket. A 10% rebate on a ticket is as yet 90% in their pocket.

For you however, you could involve these coupons for pain free income in your pocket. Assuming your manager acknowledges either the printed copy ticket receipt or the agenda, and you are permitted to utilize your own travel planner, you can utilize the coupons to help pay for your ticket. Your receipt will show the all out cost of the ticket, not the amount you really needed to pay out of pocket.

If your manager expects you to likewise show the Mastercard receipt, you'll must be more imaginative. In this situation, you'd follow through on for the ticket at full-cost, get a receipt, and afterward request that the travel planner acknowledge a coupon as a different exchange afterwards.

This equivalent cycle can be utilized to get full kudos with the expectation of complimentary tickets purchased with preferred customer credits. Pay for a refundable ticket on your credit card.

Keep your Mastercard receipt and the schedule to turn in on your cost report. Discount the ticket and afterward re-book it utilizing your preferred customer credits. Crosscountry tickets without advance buy can undoubtedly run $1800, so assuming you can do it on your preferred customer credits, it's a weighty expansion in your bank account.

Obviously, the greater part of these depart for good in the event that your organization has an in-house travel service. All things considered, I'd propose you discover which specialist is the most un-astute and attempt to talk them into imaginative bookkeeping. You might even need to pay off somebody. Travel planners don't make truckloads of money, and one may extend the organization rules to help both of you.

Double-Booking Tickets for Profit

Almost all aircrafts have PC frameworks which permit you to book however many tickets on a trip as you need. The justification for this is normal names. There could truly be five John Smith's on a flight. So in the event that you truly needed to, you could save each seat on a trip with John Doe.

If you were to book three tickets on a flight, over a time of a long time, you would probably have three distinct tolls. It ends up being undeniable that once you realized you would have been making an excursion, you could save and book a ticket. Then you wait a week before your flight and book another ticket at what is most likely a higher rate.

When you draw nearer to the flight day, drop the more extravagant, completely refundable ticket, and fly on your rebate ticket. You turn in the more extravagant receipts on your cost report.

If you use your own travel planner, they can do the discount. Assuming you have an organization based travel planner, you can in any case send the pass to the aircraft or request a discount at the air terminal counter. This will try not to warn your organization regarding what you are doing.

E-tickets make this entire cycle simpler, as the main thing you get for evidence, is the receipt from the travel planner, which is normally faxed or messaged to you. Regardless of whether you have an in-house travel planner, E-tickets are basic. When they fax you a piece a paper showing the cost and agenda of the ticket, they can't withdraw it. Regardless of whether they request it back, you copy the fax, or republish the email, it still works.

On full toll tickets and a few development tickets, you can play a cat-and-mouse game to check whether your transporter runs a deal passage bargain before you really take the flight.

Reserve the refundable charge and watch the admissions. Assuming that the transporter runs a fare

war rate, you drop the higher charge ticket (save the receipt for your cost report) and repurchase the lower admission ticket and fly on it.

The E-ticket receipting has made cost report cushioning so natural, a youngster could do it.

Flying Less and Making More Money

When you book an excursion for business and it includes more than one city, it will in all likelihood be a full toll ticket or if nothing else a completely refundable rebate ticket. At the point when you get in a circumstance like this, you can change your arrangements, hacking off the last portion or delay, and you may get a discount for the difference.

Say you're flying from Chicago to Phoenix, and associating through Denver on Monday. On Tuesday, you fly to Los Angeles. On Wednesday, you intended to fly from Los Angeles to Denver for a gathering, traveling to Chicago Thursday morning. The demonstration of "breaking" the trip in Denver adds to the expense of the ticket, when it's contrasted with a Wednesday departure from Los Angeles to Chicago, associating in Denver.

If you refer to the carrier and drop the trip as "break" in Denver, flying through Denver straightforwardly to Chicago on Wednesday, you might decrease the ticket by as much as $300. Full admission tickets are not front-end stacked like markdown tickets, so by and large all sections will convey a respectable sticker price. At the point when you appear at the counter Wednesday morning, the aircraft will credit your Visa for the distinction in the fares.

By calling the carrier before you even ticket the flights, you can check whether this technique works for your flight. Ask them, "What might occur if I..." You might even regularly add one roadtrip on your tickets, realizing you will drop the last section for profit.

Most of us could do this without disclosing to our supervisor what we did the additional last day. I'd recently fly home Wednesday and go home for the day as though I were flying back as arranged. I would get a free day away from work, in addition to the cash in my pocket. On my cost report, I'd utilize the E-ticket receipt and agenda from the first reserving and routing.

If your supervisor discovered, you could simply profess to feel sick and chose to fly home as opposed to hurling in a lodging some place. You'd say you neglected to enlighten the suitable individual regarding a day off Thursday. Assuming you would rather avoid the ailment course, you could guarantee that field-tested strategies had changed. In any case, your manager is probably not going to contemplate the reality you got cash back on the ticket.

Should I Really Be Doing This?

Airline tickets can create huge additional dollars on your cost reports, however they require exertion from you, broad preparation, and extensively more danger than a portion of the other techniques.

If somebody draws an obvious conclusion, it is difficult to shield your activities as everything except conscious. You should take some time to consider doing any of these. Assuming you have any qualms whatsoever, you ought not do them. Assuming you think there is any review trail whatsoever, you ought to keep away from them.

If your manager quits fooling around, they can generally request that the aircrafts print out a posting of what flights you really took and when. In the event that the travel planner is in-house, they can without much of a stretch think about those trips against the first directing and see what transforms you made and assuming there were any progressions in the airfare.

On the other hand, in the event that you are hoping to put a couple hundred dollars for every cost report in your pocket, carrier tickets are the most straightforward method for doing it.

One Last Review On E-tickets

This is best summarized by saying:

"Purchase and discount full tolls, involving the receipt for your cost report. Purchase and fly rebate passages, discarding the receipt afterwards."

Airline admissions change every day and a trip toward the beginning of the day can be double the charge of one more trip in the early evening. It's absolutely impossible that a manager (except if they fly similar courses frequently) can know what the best admissions are. However long your refundable charge is sensible, they in all probability won't ever address it. Assuming they do, you say, "I attempted to track down the most reduced charge, yet when I booked this flight it was the least admission I could find."

Chapter Four
How to Make Money on Hotels

Never let a travel planner book inn reservations without certain rules from you. This is the region of the booking system they know the most un-about and care about the least. Assuming that you pass on the decision to them, they will wreck it up.

Travel specialists live on commissions paid to them by the inns and carriers for reserving a spot. These add up to 10%. How long do you think they'll spend hunting, for the seven dollars your one night lodging booking gathers them?

If your organization has an in-house travel planner, they will pick the main inn which springs up on the screen which fits the organization's dollar limit strategy. There are various issues with this.

First, you have no clue about where you'll wind up. You may be twenty miles from your gathering place, on the grounds that the travel planner essentially checks out the city name. In a city like Denver, you'll have suburb urban communities like Englewood, which wander through, all through different rural areas which were shaped later.

There's a Holiday Inn ten miles out of the city, in the open country, east of Denver almost an overall flying air terminal. It's an incredible spot to remain, yet it is thirty miles from the fundamental areas of Englewood, and both appear in the travel planner's PC as Englewood.

The second thing that will happen is they'll book you in a Day's Inn, essential lodging since they thought that it is first on the rundown, when truth be told there's likewise a Hilton at the equivalent or lower rate. Your Hilton mileage credits would be lost, except if the travel planner knows your preferences.

You can save yourself a great deal of time and extra focuses the following time you stay at one of your cherished inns, by getting a registry of their areas and keeping it helpful at your office. At the point when you prepare to make a trip to a city, check whether any of them are in the town. On the off chance that they are, tell your travel planner you might want to attempt these first. They'd very much want to save themselves from hunting through the entire rundown of lodgings, on the off chance that they can observe one of your decisions inside the organization spending plan guidelines.

Check the flyers you get via the post office from the inns and carriers. Commonly there are exceptional arrangements like triple focuses for remaining at explicit inns in a city.

The travel planner might let you know they can't book you into your preferred lodging on the grounds that the PC says their rates surpass the cutoff set by the organization's cost strategy. Try not to surrender. Call the inn straightforwardly and converse with the booking agent there. Ordinarily assuming that you ask, they are running nearby exceptional rates which can get you inside the organization's guidelines.

If you don't find the solution you'd like from the booking agent, request to address the administrator. Tell them, "I would like to remain at your lodging rather than over at Hotel XYZ like my organization needs, however to do as such, you'll need to get me a similar rate." If the supervisor realizes the inn is under booked, they'll readily give you the better rate to fill a room.

You probably won't get it, yet it merits a call, especially on the grounds that the call is either on the inn's 800 number or your organization telephone. It doesn't costs anything to call, yet can assist you with getting the focuses you want.

Another thing to discover, before you show up or quickly upon your appearance, is assuming the lodging is running their own private continuous stay program.

There's a Hilton close to the air terminal in Pittsburgh, which once ran an advancement, where each dollar you spent there gave you a highlight prizes.

It wasn't restricted to the charges on your room rate as it were. It included providing food, meeting rooms, and suppers. I was doing a multi day course for 25 individuals. When every one of the charges were added up to for the stay, I accumulated 4,000 focuses. This got me a free shading TV which I still have.

There was additionally a Holiday Inn in King of Prussia, Pennsylvania which ran an advancement where every night you remained, gave you a highlight baggage, truly pleasant gear. A few lodgings will even do programs which give you dinners in their eatery or beverages at the bar. It never damages to ask.

Just as another aside, consistently inquire as to whether there are any free room updates accessible. Each inn keeps a "slush heap" of costly rooms not presently saved. Regularly, just by asking, they will overhaul you to no end extra. This will most frequently occur assuming that you are going through only one evening. I realize this doesn't appear to seem OK, yet let me explain to you why they do this.

When the inn gets down to only a couple of rooms left and Thusmebody calls without a second to spare, they can undoubtedly sell the lower estimated rooms. Most latest possible moment guests went up against with paying large dollars for a suite will in all likelihood call somewhere else to track down a superior rate. So, in the event that the inn can redesign you to the more costly room and keep a couple of lower evaluated spaces for those last moment reservations, they can and will do it.

How to Get Blank Hotel Receipts

Getting clear receipts from inns is genuinely simple to do. Many are nonexclusive, in that they have the inn network's logo and work space address and such on it, however the residential location telephone number is imprinted on the receipt by their PC when you check out.

Most organization's will acknowledge the receipt from the lodging, without the back up of your real charge card receipt. The justification behind this, is most inn PCs will print at the lower part of the receipt, "Settled completely" or it will print, "Paid with Credit Card #123456".

If this fulfills your chief and records payable office, you can in a real sense compose your own receipts on your home PC or a typewriter, on the off chance that you have some clear receipt paper.

The least demanding method for getting the genuine clear structures, is to just request it. At the point when you are looking at in or, notice to the agent, "Hello, I truly like the format of your receipt paper. I'm certain my supervisor might want to check whether the organization would work for our organization. May I have a couple of sheets to reclaim with me?" Most assistants will simply hand them over to you.

If they can't or will not do that, there is another way. Commonly, while stacking their printer, the lodging squanders a couple of sheets adjusting the structures. The agents now and again utilize these for scratch paper. You could as well. What you do, is act somewhat confounded at the counter and afterward request one of the sheets to take a couple notes.

Failing the above strategies, there is generally the old backup strategy for going through the junk. The evening group generally is the person who gathers the junk and replaces the plastic packs in the workplace garbage cans. They regularly stack the sacks outside of the indirect access prompting the workplace, so a janitor can get them in the morning.

No one watches them well. This is awful, as this is presumably the most continuous technique hoodlums use to get utilized charge card slips so they can utilize your number. I don't approve it. Oddly enough, I see nothing ethically amiss with ripping off my organization through cost reports, however utilizing another person's charge card number isn't reasonable for individual travelers.

If you want clear receipt structures from the lodging, you could "get" one sack to the point of scavenging through it for the paper you want.

How to Get the Hotel to Print Fake Receipts

I realize it sounds insane, yet assuming you know how, you can get the inn to print faked or swelled receipts for you, and they will not realize they are doing it.

Every time you reserve a spot, the inn or the public reservation administration will statement you a rate and enter it into your booking record. The agents have in a real sense many rates accessible to cite. There are rates for the AARP, the AAA, IBM, and surprisingly the NBA. There are rates for seniors, youngsters, and likely even sophomores. The fact of the matter is, there are many rates other than the one you were cited, accessible for the asking.

If you realize you are qualified for suppose an AAA markdown on the grounds that you have a place with the auto club, don't let them know when you reserve the spot. Allow them to book you in at the typical "rack" rate. Before you show up, call the inn and ask somebody what the AAA rate is. Note their name, the date you asked, and the rate.

If you have an in-house travel planner, don't enlighten them concerning your unique markdown openings. Allow them to book your lodging at their corporate rate and

then call the inn to check whether your markdown is better, and afterward attempt this strategy.

At the point when you check in, the lodging will ordinarily circle the rate on the booking card and request that you introductory it. They need you to do this, so there is no question when you look at with respect to what rate you would have been charged, which is by and large what it is you need to do.

The agents are not generally perceptive once they give you the card, particularly assuming they are occupied. In the first place, attempt not initialing the rate. Assuming they don't get it, you're good to go. Assuming they get it and ask you again to beginning it, feel free to introductory it, yet in something else altogether than you typically would.

The way in to this stunt is the way that the representative who actually look at you in, late in the evening one evening, isn't a similar assistant who looks at you the following morning. What you need to do in the first part of the day, is get them to print a duplicate of your bill for assessment. In practically all lodgings, this will be your receipt assuming that there are no objections.

When they give you the charge, you debate the rate. You are furnished with such a lot of data now, they can not contend it, in spite of the fact that they will attempt. You can see them, "Hello, this should be the AAA rate. I conversed with this and that, on this date, and they cited this rate."

That assertion alone, upheld with such a lot of truth, will typically be to the point of getting them to re-print you the remedied and lower estimated receipt. Your unique, more extravagant receipt goes in your pocket to be submitted with your cost report. Ten dollars each day less for a five night stay will permit you to get an additional a $50 in addition to charges from your employer.

If the representative attempts to uphold the ,"...you initialed the rate on the card when you checked in..." contention, you can show them you didn't beginning the card, if indeed you didn't. Assuming that you did with the uncommon initialing, you can say, "Another person more likely than not initialed this, since I sure didn't. This is the way I beginning things."

If you create sufficient uproar, serenely and coolly, you will quite often get the re-print. Assuming that they actually reject, it is all the same to of you, in light of the fact that the organization will repay you at the full cost. You simply will not have the option to get the additional money... TODAY!

The battle is as yet not finished assuming the inn closes you out. You can in any case compose their corporate office and guarantee they distorted their rate, that they were inconsiderate and uncooperative, and whatever it takes to make them sound like monstrosities. An inn's corporate office will quite often send you a refund.

Sometimes, you can guiltlessly wind up doing This two rate switch. This happens when they neglect to get the right rate on the booking card and you're checking in extremely late. The supervisor is clearly not working, so assuming you have a rate question, there is typically nothing that should be possible until the following day.

Ask the agent to note on the enlistment card that the rate is disputed. When you look at, let them print the wrong bill, and really at that time request that they settle the debate and once again print the bill.

Another minor method of getting a more extravagant bill to submit, includes the fifty to 75 penny charges which are frequently added per call on your bill. This should be for nearby calls, however a few inns charge this for each cordial call, even 800 numbers. Assuming you do a ton of calls, this can be five or ten bucks for every day.

When you look at and after they have printed your receipt, request to have these charges eliminated from your bill. This is absolutely at their impulse, however on the off chance that you are firm and intense, you can get them postponed. The recently re-printed bill will be lower and you turn in the higher one for your cost report.

Some other minor advantages which lodgings accommodate you include room-administration. By and by, this closely relates to receipts and being firm.

The primary advantage is room administration for the most part shows up with a receipt which likewise has a detach receipt at the base. Some of the time these receipts have the lodging logo on them. That is OK, it will in any case function as a receipt on another dinner. Assuming the receipt really has the inn's extravagant café logo on it, that is perfect.

Sign the receipt over to your room bill, so you pay for it as a section on your inn receipt, a passage for use on your cost report. The detach receipt is currently a clear one you can involve later and place for verification of a feast purchased.

The other advantage takes nerve. In the event that your feast is extremely late in showing up or they convey some unacceptable supper, call the kitchen supervisor and request a discount for the dinner. Regardless of whether the food is incredible, you could call and grumble and get it free or diminished. The charge shouldn't hit your lodging bill as it occurred in a similar charging period, however you actually have the detach receipt to turn in later as an expense.

How far you need to take these methods is dependent upon you and your conscience.

Chapter Five

How to Make Money on Rental Cars

This most probable will be the briefest section in the book, as making cash on rental vehicles with your cost report is the most troublesome stunt to do. A piece of this has to do with the refinement of the PC frameworks the greater part of the significant rental organizations presently use.

Almost every rental office utilizes the remote printing PC hand-sets to finish your charging when you return a rental vehicle. This joined with the profoundly computerized rental methodology of the booking clubs, which preprint your agreement, leaves practically zero wiggle room or human intervention.

To bring in genuine cash on a rental vehicle requires more out right unscrupulousness and exertion from you. The dangers related with this, and the time squandered to pull them off, may not be worth it.

I'm not exactly certain how rental vehicle organizations got so close with their methods around here, since, supposing that you check out their general activity, their strategies in each of different regions are terrible.

Most of you who travel much by any means, should go along with one or all of the rental vehicle offices reservation clubs. They all work about something very similar. You finish up a profile which the organization keeps in their PC and they issue you an ID number.

When you hold a vehicle, they access your record, and preprint a tenant agreement at the hour of your appearance. The profile lets them know the class of vehicle you need, and it lets them know what exceptional agreement valuing arrangements are essentially, and what Visa to charge for the rental.

In principle, you show up at the air terminal and go straightforwardly to the transport which takes you to the rental parcel. At the point when you arrive, your name is on a board which lets you know where your vehicle is left. Your vehicle is prepared with the agreement normally holding tight the rearview reflect. In the colder time of year, they in some cases have the vehicle heated going for you.

I have horrible karma with these projects. I frequently travel twenty weeks every year and make stops in a few urban communities each outing, so I lease a great deal of vehicles. In specific urban communities, similar to Chicago, I can ensure my vehicle is rarely prepared. Assuming that it will be, it is either some unacceptable vehicle, it's running on empty, a tire is level, or the battery is dead.

Since I have the room, let me caution you of a couple of malicious stunts the rental vehicle offices do to get more cash out of you. Assuming that you are perusing this book, you may not mind at all assuming the organization pays more, yet for your own rentals, you'll need to know about these.

Most of the significant offices offer a type of fuel choice. They attempt to unnerve you into purchasing this choice by notice you, "Assuming you return the vehicle with under a full tank, we'll charge you $50 a gallon to fill it."

I realize this is a misrepresentation, however they don't make you hang tight for them to fill your tank and charge you for the missing gas. They charge you dependent on the miles driven or an allocated computation dependent on the sum appearing on the fuel measure. They once in a while charge you as much as 20 pennies for each mile driven. In a minimal vehicle, this can be more than $5 a gallon.

They let you that know if you pre-pay for a full tank of gas, for the most part at a rate they guarantee is a dime or two beneath nearby costs, you can carry the vehicle back with the tank unfilled and they won't charge you. What they don't tell you, is they likewise won't discount the cash assuming you bring the vehicle back half full or full. Except if you're great or like facing challenges, you will carry the vehicle back with a respectable measure of gas actually left in the tank. You paid for gas you didn't utilize, and that is free cash to them.

Another stunt they like to do, is discussion you into a redesign at your cost.

This occurs in offices which actually make you go to the counter to lease a vehicle. It in all likelihood happens in more modest urban communities, yet I have had somebody give this a shot me in Houston. At the point when you check in, they'll say they can update you to a higher degree of vehicle for several dollars a day.

Again, this is all the more free cash to them. They're relying on the reality you couldn't care less assuming you put in a couple of a greater amount of the organization's dollars. Indeed, the representatives are generally given a reward for each update they can sell.

The essential trouble with utilizing the rental vehicle to produce cost report income, is that your receipt is printed at the outright finish of your exchange, after a few designated spots have happened. It's difficult to guarantee you didn't have the vehicle you had, when you are appearing with it to check in for the receipt. Moreover, when there is an issue and a receipt should be transformed, they are over the top about getting your duplicate of the wrong receipt back from you.

It should be possible yet it will slow you up, both looking at in and, as the main genuine method for doing it will require human intercession. I would propose it does not merit your time, as the human consider working the vehicle rental world is truly poor. They are slow, they are firm, and they would rather not help. Their entire framework is intended to make human to human contact a special case for the rule.

How to Get What You Can

One region where you may pull off receipt altering, includes coupons for limits. This will commonly just work on those which have fixed dollar sums off of the rental. Now and then you can move away with

utilizing the get one day, get one day free coupons. To utilize them, you must be firm and perhaps obnoxious.

You return your vehicle like typical, get your receipt, and afterward stroll into the workplace where you would get the transport for the outing back to the air terminal. On the off chance that you attempt to hand the coupon to the individual really looking at you in at the vehicle, they'll concede printing you a receipt and allude you inside for help. You really want them to print you a receipt BEFORE they send you to the office.

You need to stroll, close by them your coupon and guarantee there's been a mistake. You say, "I let them know when I reserved the spot that I had this coupon and they should check my record for the agreement. They let me know I'd need to hand the coupon in when I returned the vehicle. Presently I'm told I can't utilize it."

If you push sufficiently, you can get them to credit your charge card for how much the coupon and potentially let you keep the receipt from the first printout. This requires some investment and energy, which can be totally squandered on the off chance that they take the receipt.

The main genuine choice you have is to totally counterfeit a receipt utilizing calculator tape through your spot network printer or on a typewriter. You must be great to do it. You start with a real receipt and duplicate the organization. There's a huge load of data encoded on the receipt and you must be exceptionally exact with your data assuming that you need it to look legitimate.

What Other Areas Can I Use to Get Money

Fortunately, there are different areas of rental vehicle use which can be utilized for your cost report, which are more straightforward to counterfeit or overstate. One of those is a gas receipt.

For the majority of us, we can discount the fuel utilized in the rental vehicle. There is no standard organization for the gas stations around the country, taking everything into account. In the event that you utilize the programmed charge card islands at the corner store, you'll lock yourself out, however assuming you pay inside, you have a great deal of flexibility.

Some more seasoned service stations leave a book or pile of clear receipts close to the sales register for you to take on the off chance that you really want one. Corner store specialists truly prefer not to finish up receipts, particularly on the off chance that you just put a dollar or two of gas in the car.

Some service stations conceal the structures, yet they will hand-compose the sum on what should be a charge card receipt. Assuming they hand-compose a dollar or two, including a one front of it makes it eleven or twelve dollars. Ensure you turn in the duplicate, as they can not follow the two unique shades of ink that way. Assuming you're not happy with that a very remarkable error, one dollar can become seven effectively, especially on the carbon copy.

Another thing to ponder with corner stores is to look for the receipts of others who didn't take them with them. This is extremely kind with oneself serve Visa islands, as a many individuals take their receipt and then toss it in the waste. A brief glance in the canister may get you a PC printed receipt for a very long time more than you are paying. These are magnificent on the grounds that they will convey the name of the corner store, possibly the city name, and a period/date stamp which matches your movement plans.

Some service stations utilize only a customary sales register receipt for gas just as food and brew. Check out the counter and check whether any individual who purchased an instance of brew, abandoned the receipt. You can involve it for your cost report.

The main conceivable issue you have in this space springs up assuming your rental vehicle receipt shows the quantity of miles driven. On the off chance that you turn in a gas receipt for ten gallons worth of gas and you traveled fifteen miles, you could have an issue. This is genuinely simple to cover, by asserting the return representative entered some unacceptable mileage by dropping 100 miles in the calculation.

Trying to be reasonable, there are various authentic motivations behind why there might be a sizable hole between the mileage driven and gallons purchased. Commonly, the individual who leased the vehicle before you will travel twenty miles and return the vehicle without topping off the tank, guaranteeing they did. You get a vehicle which is as of now down a gallon or two.

Exactly the same thing can happen to you, in the event that you lease from an office who purposefully "shorts" the tank by a gallon while setting up the vehicle for rental. A few rental areas do this. If they save themselves a gallon per rental, times a thousand rentals a day, it adds up nicely for them.

Finally, vehicle mileage can change from the thirty or more miles for each gallon on a GEO Metro, to the fifteen miles for every gallon of a Lincoln Continental. Along these lines, except if your rental receipt has a vehicle type referenced, some variety is expected.

Parking is another region which you might have the option to cushion by getting stray receipts or adding digits to the sum. Assuming you are qualified for guarantee a sensible measure of stopping on your cost report, you can get a couple of bucks here and there.

Some parking structures give hands down the barest of receipts, a basic sales register tape which just shows the sum tended. These make it simple, as they only here and there have dates or times on them, so you can search for others lounging around with higher amounts.

Those leaving offices who utilize the PC created receipts can be faked like rental vehicle receipts to imitate them on your PC or on a typewriter. The right sorts of paper including the substance duplicate kinds of paper can be found at the workplace supply store.

One other region which is available to the attentiveness of your organization or chief, includes cash utilized for stopping meters or costs. You can't visit region of the nation like Chicago or Pennsylvania without managing tollgates on the streets. These quite often work on a money just premise and getting receipts from some is darned close impossible.

If your organization or supervisor permits you to present a sum without receipts for costs and coin worked stopping, then, at that point, you can clearly expand the sums above what you really spent.

Car Related Expenses

This is the best spot I can imagine to manage two issues. Both are connected with mileage repayment for the business utilization of your own vehicle. One is being paid by your boss for utilizing your vehicle on business, and the other is utilizing a rental vehicle as opposed to utilizing your own vehicle, for business.

The IRS permits you to be repaid by your manager a specific sum for each mile for the business utilization of your own vehicle. Organization strategies only here and there pay the full IRS sum, however they approach. The IRS sum changes from one year to another occasionally. Contingent on how your own expenses are taken care of, you might have the option to recover the distinction on your taxes.

For the purpose of this contention, we should accept your boss repays you a quarter for each mile, when you use your vehicle for business. The primary clear reality, is you can undoubtedly add miles without your manager discovering. There are generally products of courses between two places, just as the requirement for minimal side outings and tasks once you are at your destination.

If you travel just a 1000 miles absolute for boss a year, you actually could presumably add one more 200 miles without raising any doubt. This additional mileage would give you another $50. It isn't huge dollars, however it is free cash. Assuming you use your vehicle more than that, say 5000 miles each year, you could without much of a stretch conceal one more 1000 miles for a raise of $250.

Now we should take a gander at another situation. Suppose your supervisor needs you to

drive to a business meeting in another town 360 miles away. With the full circle, coincidental outings, and tasks, you could most likely rack up almost 1000 miles for the excursion. In the event that you really drive 750 and your vehicle gets 30 miles for every gallon, you'd spend about $32 on gas, regardless of whether you drive your vehicle or a rental car.

You will consume the gas and put these additional miles on your vehicle, causing mileage which deteriorates your vehicle. Assuming the gathering is a three roadtrip, you could have a go at leasing a vehicle and not telling your chief. You could presumably lease a vehicle for under $40 per day, so your rental would add up to $120.

For the 1000 miles you are going in to your manager, you will be paid $250. You will save the mileage on your vehicle, in addition to take $130. Your manager doesn't really mind whose vehicle you drive, just that you are there for the gathering. The following time you need to take a sizable drive for your manager, crunch the numbers and check whether you can leave your own vehicle at home.

Chapter Six
Making Money on Meals and Entertainment

If there at any point was a region on a cost report uniquely designed for misuse; dinners and amusement is the one. No other region of the cost report has so little control by outside offices thus much control in your grasp. You are in complete control of the process.

You select where you eat. You can handle who you take out for lunch and where you go. You choose if you will eat one, two, or three suppers each day. Just you control the realities expected to back your cases for repayment on your cost report.

The truly sweet thing about this area of operational expense, is you can do it with the high level information and authorization of the chief. Getting earlier endorsement makes things such a great deal simpler to stow away or expand. Go to your chief and say, "You know, it very well may be really smart to take the buying specialist from ABC Bowling Supply out to supper. I figure I'll do that one week from now. Would it be a good idea for me to welcome her better half?"

Your chief, will no doubt concur, and advise you to welcome the companion. Presently you have a limitless ticket to ride to do anything you desire. You could turn in receipts as though you took both of them and your life partner to supper and pocket the entire feast. You might need to take just the buying specialist to supper, yet turn in a receipt with four individuals of dinners. You could take your own affection interest to an extravagant eatery, and turn the receipt in as though it were four individuals at a sensible restaurant.

The blends might be unending here, however the point is self-evident, as long

as your supervisor isn't with you, you can make up whatever story you need.

Methods Involving Your Personal Meals

You are qualified for eat while you are out and about. Your manager might pay you as an outlay for suppers or permit you to discount real charges. Your boss might draw dollar lines per supper or an every day all out limit for all meals.

Whatever they do, you have the scope to make a ton of money.

If you are on an outlay, you want to oversee things to get however many free or modest dinners as could be allowed so you can stash the distinction. What to consider is the inn where you stay on your trip.

Many of the inn networks offer a free breakfast as a feature of your room rate. These are normally a mainland breakfast, which means you get rolls, doughnuts, juice and some espresso. At certain properties, the morning meal can incorporate toaster oven waffles, oats, organic product, and surprisingly a few breakfast meats. Assuming the inn has a considerable breakfast, you might have the option to skip lunch by having a major breakfast. You could two or three bits of organic product with you, or a granola bar or two, to eat for lunch.

If you can convince another person to get you lunch, you set aside your outlay cash. You may even get sufficiently frantic to consent to lunch with a seller or salesperson. It's smarter to pay attention to an attempt to close the deal you would rather not hear than to pay for a lunch out of your pocket.

Notwithstanding breakfast, a few lodgings offer a "Party time" with appetizers in the evening. Some have a sufficient spread, that it effectively could be made into a supper. Loading up on mixed drink weinies, tacos, or vegetables with plunge can limit the requirement for a supper. Assuming you have a major breakfast, bring along some natural product for lunch, and eat a major plate of tidbits, you could get by without spending any of your outlay for meals.

Another interesting point, in the event that you are on a routine set of expenses, is to remain at an inn which has a little kitchen or full kitchen in your room. Assuming you have a fridge and microwave, you could without much of a stretch cook your own dinners. Cooking for yourself can be exceptionally modest and more solid than eating in restaurants.
Anything you save versus your routine set of expenses, is cash in your bank account.

If you get to utilize real receipts, you can pull off murder. The primary stunt is getting receipts. Figure out how to gather them. On the off chance that you can't gather them, stop by the nearby office supply store and get a bundle of receipts with the detach bottoms. What you must be cautious with on the detach receipts, is they accompanied chronic numbers imprinted on them. Try not to be sufficiently senseless to involve three receipts in continuous request on the equivalent report.

You can undoubtedly gather a colossal store of these clear receipts, as they can be tracked down out of control. Each time you elapse an eatery at an inn, approach the host or master and say, "I ate here yesterday and neglected to get a receipt, would I be able to have one off of the lower part of a receipt." They'll forever give you one or two.

If you see receipts sitting from different supporters, grab them up for use by you later. On the off chance that you see additional receipts sitting close to the sales register, pick them up. At the point when you pay with a Mastercard for a supper, the first request structure utilized by the server most likely had a detach receipt on it. Save the receipt for later and utilize the Mastercard receipt, or utilize the remove receipt to report a more costly supper than what you ate and paid for.

One of my cherished stunts in this space can best be exampled by an excursion through O'Hare air terminal in Chicago. On the off chance that you eat at one of the café and go through the look at line, the representative will give you a receipt. Assuming that you bring down your eyes a foot or two, you'll see a heap of different receipts left behind by different supporters, at the foundation of the money register.

If you snatch a small bunch and go through them, you'll unavoidably observe receipts which are for sums bigger than whatever you spent. You keep the most costly one you find, and turn it in on your cost report. The magnificence of this is the receipt has the name of the air terminal, the date, and the time. You are qualified for eat while out and about. You're honestly at a similar spot, simultaneously, on a similar date as you are relied upon to be. It turns into the ideal swelled receipt.

Some businesses won't acknowledge detach receipt, and will compose strategies to limit their utilization. In a previous part I covered how to get around this with your chief, however there are alternate ways of getting your boss to acknowledge the remove receipt more easily.

Sometimes managers will feel more good assuming an eatery worker marked the front of the detach receipt. You could clearly manufacture counterfeit marks assuming you needed, however it would be more secure to ask a companion or a mate to fill in the sum, sign ,and date the receipt for you. That way, it is absolutely impossible that the mark resembles yours and assuming you're inquired as to whether you finished it up, you can genuinely say, "No."

If your manager permits you to turn in the real receipts up to we should say

$40 each day, you could do the accompanying. Have the mainland breakfast at the lodging and turn in $4.76 on a detach receipt for breakfast. Skip lunch and turn in $9.88 on one more remove receipt. Eat the party time snacks at the hotel

that evening and turn in one more receipt for the $23.86 "supper" you didn't eat.

You'll gather $38.50 for dinners for which you didn't eat or pay. Do this every day on a five roadtrip and pocket an additional a $192.50 for the outing. Do this twenty weeks per year and bring home an additional a $3850. That is a pre-charge increase in salary of more than $6400.

To be protected, you ought to presumably change the sums essentially and perhaps skirt a supper or two to make it appear to be unique. You can in any case ensure your absolute dollar sum, by turning in a morning meal for $9, skip lunch, and turn in a supper of $28. You get the difference in your example which confounds your chief, you actually draw near to as far as possible for the day.

Something last to ponder. Suppose you are going on a work excursion to Las Vegas or New Orleans. The organization is paying for your airfare, rental vehicle, and inn. On the off chance that you utilize a portion of your preferred customer credits, a life partner or companion could go with you on the outing free of charge. This set-up is particularly great assuming you volunteer to fly on a Sunday to save the organization on the airfare.

In Las Vegas, you two could undoubtedly devour buffet morning meals and prime rib suppers and still be inside your every day dollar limits for your very own dinners. You essentially turn the receipt in as though it was your dinner alone. In numerous different towns, you could in any case eat at unassuming cafés inside those cutoff points. Regardless, the organization would be paying for your own vacation.

Cashing In On Lunch and Dinner With Others

If you have the leeway to purchase lunch as well as supper for other people, you altogether grow how much room you need to add costs to your pocketbook.

Your manager won't call somebody you guarantee to have taken to lunch to check whether you truly did. There are not many things your manager could do which would be more dumb than that. Assuming it is a client; your chief, your organization, and you would lose everything credibility.

You should kiss off any way to at any point work with that individual or firm once more. Regardless of whether it was authentic and you had taken them to lunch, the reality your supervisor called to check, annihilates all believability your organization has with that client. I don't think any supervisor is that stupid.

If my manager could at any point inquire as to whether I took them to lunch or supper, I'd go through the rooftop. I would stop on the spot and tell my manager I'm suing the organization. Regardless of whether the doubt were advocated, nothing subverts your notoriety with a customer more, than having your chief "looking up" on you. No appointed authority will be thoughtful with a supervisor who did that.

Now that we have this on the table, it normally follows you can pull off a sensible measure of imaginary amusement. Simply be certain you don't really have taken Bob Smith to lunch around the same time your manager turns out to golf with Bob Smith. That one is excessively obvious.

Saying you took somebody to lunch or supper, when you didn't buy lunch or supper yourself, is doubly great for your funds. You pocket two suppers worth of money from your cost report. Saying you celebrated two others is triply really great for the bank account.

I'm losing trace of what's most important here. Somebody years prior let me know something which seems OK. They said, "When you're out and about, you must eat. You should ask somebody out for a business lunch, and eat for free."

That's an illustration I've will always remember. Assuming business routine incorporates the capacity to take others to lunch, you can eat free of charge. Albeit this doesn't place cash into your pocket, it saves you from spending your own cash for lunch. Assuming you would regularly burn through $5 on yourself for lunch and you'd do this 200 days every year, you save yourself $1000 by purchasing another person lunch as a business expense.

Now the subsequent stage in heightening your pay is to have the business lunch, yet with another person who will turn it on their cost report. Clearly this works best with somebody from another organization. They cost your dinner, however on your cost report you present a receipt as though you had purchased the lunch. You had lunch for nothing, setting aside your own cash, in addition to the organization will repay you for both snacks you didn't buy. That resembles getting triple pay.

Another truly smooth method of taking a great deal of money, is to sort out for a genuinely enormous gathering of individuals, suppose ten, to meet at an eatery after work for somebody's birthday or commemoration. You make it clear to everybody that they are all alone, however that you will "run a tab" to make it advantageous for the gathering, on your charge card. Toward the finish of the evening, everybody pays you their portion in real money. You have a real receipt to use on your cost report. Regardless of whether the social event is a moderate ten dollars a head, you got $100 cash from them, and you'll gather $110 when you turn in the receipt.

Never forget the program on your charge card, where taking part eateries discount as much as 20% of the dinner to you in an actually take a look at every month. Not exclusively would you be able to gather two times for the dinner, yet you'll get one more twenty bucks through the mail.

Another memorable thing is despite the fact that it isn't cash in your pocket, suppers paid for by the organization saves you from spending your own well deserved money. For example, how does your manager know the business supper you purchased final evening was a customer and not an adoration interest of yours? Taking a beau or sweetheart to supper at a five star café can have other incidental advantages to you. It's that greatly improved assuming the organization is paying for the meal.

Golf, The Final Frontier

Lunches and suppers are not by any means the only sort of business diversion organizations will permit you to discount. Passes to the theater, games, or nearby celebrations are frequently utilized as deals impetuses. Taking your customer hitting the fairway, hunting, fishing, or drifting is normal. Later in this part, I'll cover gifts exhaustively, however a ton of business is purchased each year with corporate presents to customers.

Those of you who don't golf, have no clue about the number of business openings have been lost to you. Whether or not you partake in the game, there are not many different exercises where you can get a business customer, one on one as a basically enthralled crowd as you can during a five hour round of golf. A leader who won't allow you five minutes in their office, will go the entire day with you assuming you are "punishing the white ball" on the fairway at your expense.

I immovably accept all that business exhortation that a college can provide for every one of its understudies is, "Go forward and foster a decent short game." So much enormous business is led and arrangements concluded on the greens of the United States, that business colleges should make golf a necessary subject in their curricula.

For you, the advantages of being a golf player with a task which permits you to discount golf excursions, is totally superb. The primary advantage is private. On the off chance that you can go through a day seven days hitting the fairway for nothing at the organization's cost, you getting a free vacation day unwinding in the daylight accomplishing something you love.

The subsequent advantage can be monetary reserve funds, as in getting another person to pay for your golf expenses, possibly free golf balls and golf shirts with the organization logo, and lunch at the tidbit shop. Hitting the fairway isn't modest. A fair golf excursion for two can without much of a stretch amount to $100. At prime fairways, the benevolent the organization's leaders like to play, a similar excursion can run as much as $500. Regardless of whether you were playing without anyone else once per week at a public course, getting the organization to pay simply your greens expenses would by and by save you $1500 a year.

A third advantage is the capacity to play golf and pocket a ton of money. A few customers, as a result of their organization's standards, will demand paying for their own golf expenses. Assuming you get to the green early and pre-pay the charges for both of you, you can get the customer to pay you their portion and still cost the whole excursion on your cost report. To truly push it, you can profess to golf with somebody or a gathering, when indeed you are hitting the fairway alone. You cost for an imaginary foursome when you have really paid for one.

Golf is by all accounts a region where you can persuade your supervisor to undermine their cost report. On the off chance that they are likewise a golf player, you can in some cases get your supervisor to consent to a green gathering. This has the advantage of the "holding custom", where you become golf pals. Most organizations won't permit associates to discount a lot of anything, particularly golf excursions. Be that as it may, your supervisor might consent to have you pay for the round of golf and turn it in on your cost report as though YOU took out a client.

Why and how might your manager need to do this? It's basic actually. Most organizations utilize an endorsement cycle called "one more than one" for cost reports. I turn in a cost report and my manager is the main endorsement required. Assuming my supervisor turns in a cost report, their manager is the main endorsement required. In the event that my manager needs both of us to go playing golf without raising the doubts of their chief, they make me pay for itself and put it in on my cost report. The manager endorses my cost report and no other person is the wiser.

This has twofold advantages for you. To pay for your golf so you two can discuss work, that is incredible for you. Even better, you have proof of your supervisor undermining their cost report. It will become hard for them to train you for a rashness, when you have evidence of their cheating.

Aside from the genuine excursions, there are numerous different advantages to you.

Companies love to offer golf balls with their logo on them. It resembles free publicizing hiding in woods, lakes and terraces all over America. Golf shirts, umbrellas, divot apparatuses, towels, and even golf sacks can be embellished with the organization logo. Clearly intended to be gifts to customers, it is likewise vital for you to have them to "show your organization soul" out on the course. These are on the whole supplies you didn't need to purchase with your own money.

Meals Are Not The Only Form of Entertainment

Tickets to neighborhood sports groups, proficient in the event that you live in a major city, are exceptionally famous with clients. To make the buy advantageous, it's

fundamental for you to come to the game with the customer. All things considered, you can not talk business with a client except if you are there to speak.

Your manager might permit you to regularly purchase these tickets for clients. In the event that you do a great deal of it, you might have the option to persuade your manager to allow you to discount season tickets, as they're less expensive all the time than purchasing individual tickets for each game.

You benefit in various ways assuming you can do this. To begin with, you get to go to the games in general in the event that you decide. Second, you're not going to have a customer accessible for each game, so you can treat companions and family members at the organization's cost. Third, assuming you choose not to go to the "main round of the period", you could scalp your tickets for cash. Different advantages with season tickets are favored stopping, better seats, moves up to far and away superior seats as they become accessible every year, and favored determination for purchasing passes to play-off games.

Theater tickets are likewise extraordinary corporate presents for customers. These can be purchased as season tickets too, at extraordinary "reserve funds" to the organization. In the event that you live in a bigger city where Broadway-type shows regularly visit, this can be costly. Assuming you go to see a voyaging Broadway show, great seats effectively cost $75 each. By getting the organization to get a few tickets and going with the customer to "make it worth our time and energy", you can go to the show free of charge, perhaps including supper previously or after the show. On the off chance that for reasons unknown the customer "drops" on you, you could scalp the tickets for cash.

I could continue forever with models, as the areas of dinners and diversion are awesome and most straightforward method for taking advantage of your cost report. Any remaining techniques for trading out, are minor departure from the ones I just gave you. Around here, the receipt prerequisites differ colossally and the capacity to follow realities is seriously limited.

Meetings, Conventions, and Seminars, Oh My!

If you are at any point engaged with arranging courses and shows for your organization, an immense new field of double-dealing is accessible for you to utilize and mishandle. Regular situations for which these regions are accessible are deals, promoting, the executives, and even secretaries and clerical specialists. Any individual who needs to purchase presents, prizes, supplies and those limited time materials for the shows, can take advantage of these functions.

If you are one of the organizers for a huge course, your manager has given you the capacity to use the granting of immense lumps of business, similar to lodgings and catering, to the most noteworthy bidder. In reality, your manager is looking

for the most minimal bidders for the administrations. You are searching for the most elevated bidder for yourself.

If you are arranging an arrangement with inns to hold a class in their office, which will have handfuls or even many participants, you hold the handbag strings on thousands, possibly countless dollars of business. Shouldn't you get something from a lodging or conference hall for turning the business their way?

You don't set yourself up to request cash pay-offs from the sellers. Your manager would observe that one out instantly and you'll get thrown out with the waste. In any case, you could "hint" to the merchants that you have certain “needs” which could be “unexpectedly” dealt with by the individuals who are “grateful” of the business we’ve done in the past.

What does that mean? At the point when you’re arranging the arrangement and tolerating offers, you be quite certain with the merchants. Let them know your organization arrangements are to such an extent that you can not acknowledge tips, either in real money or presents for coordinating business their way.

However, you can specify connections you’ve had with sellers, before, who in appreciation for the business you’ve led with them, surprised you with presents at Christmas time or your birthday. Those obliging individuals have a “unique spot” in your heart.

Let me be specific. A hotel chain can give you some free dinners at little or no cost to themselves. They could give you certificates for free nights at any of their hotels, anywhere in the country. If the contract was large enough, the gifts might exceed these.

The important point, to avoid real problems with your company, is these gifts must “come from out of the blue” without an obvious connection. If it happens that way, you could go to your boss and show what they want to give you and ask, “I’m not really comfortable with this, but is it okay for me to use them?” Your boss will probably say yes. (Unless they want to take them from you and use them for their own.)

When your company rents a booth at a trade show, there is almost always a need to give away prizes in a raffle or drawing, in order to get people to stop by your booth. If you are the person asked to buy the prizes, why not buy something you’d like to have yourself?

Let’s say you are sent out to buy “prizes” for the drawing. Your boss is unlikely to be one of the people populating the booth at the convention. Therefore, if you personally needed say, a camera, you could buy four prizes, keep one for yourself and raffle off the other three. If your boss sets a total dollar limit for the prizes, you can still arrange the distribution so that your personal selection is the most expensive.

If you want to add a safety margin to doing this, it would be easy to do. Buy the four prizes. Keep the one you want in your office and raffle off the other three at the convention. Turn in your expense report and wait for it to be paid. If they pay the report without incident and another thirty days go by, you’re probably past any questions.

If on the other hand, someone puts two and two together and asks you about the extra prize, you can open your desk drawer and say, “I thought three prizes were enough to give away, so I thought we’d save this one for the next convention.” No harm, no foul.

How far you push your luck in this area depends completely on how many people will have visibility to the prizes being awarded. If once the prizes are awarded, no one cares or knows who won, you can get away with quite a bit. If you have to publicly list or announce who won what, there's too much visibility and lasting evidence to risk too much.

Chapter Seven
What To Do If You Get Caught

As one of the final chapters, I found it necessary to discuss what to do if you get caught cheating on your expense report. Before I do this, I think we really should revisit the moral questions involved with whether or not you cheat.

As the first chapter of this book warned, if you want to go through life squeaky clean and never have anything that might blemish your record or conscience, do not do any of the things in this book.

The principles in this book are like a drug. The more you use them, the more you want to use them. Once you get away with five dollars, you'll want to try for fifty. You have to be very careful these ideas do not lead you into "harder" crimes against your employer.

Those of you who are fans of Star Wars movies will remember the discussions about the powers of the "force" and an admonishment to "beware the dark side" of the force. Specifically, the warning goes, "Beware the power of the dark side of the force. Once you start down that path, forever will it dominate your life." That's the way it is with padding your expense report. Once you start, there's little incentive to stop.

The more practical argument involved with whether or not you do this, is the possibility of losing your job. Some employers find absolutely no margin for error in such matters. Some employers will fire people if they take a box of ink pens home. They have a "no tolerance" policy in such matters. If you are found padding your expense report with even one breakfast or taxi cab receipt, you could be tossed out the door.

You have to be very careful to balance the value of your on-going employment with the extra bucks you are trying to get. I've seen it happen a dozen times in my career. I've seen a Vice President fired for accepting golf clubs from a vendor in exchange for awarding a small contract for parts. All the people in the company had the same reaction. They asked, "Why would he jeopardize a $100,000 a year job for a set of golf clubs?"

If you get caught padding your expense report, they could be asking, "Why'd they risk their reputation and job, for twenty dollars?" Before you try anything in this book, think long and hard. If you never cheat on your expense report, you have nothing to fear.

Now, let's look at the other side of reality. If the management wants you out the door, they will find something to pin it on. Making accusations against you on your expense report is an easy way to do it. It would be very easy for them to pull your last ten or twenty expense reports and go over it with a fine toothed comb. They can claim you added extra mileage. They can claim you turned in a breakfast receipt when you didn't. They can claim you did not take Betty Jones out to lunch when you said you did.

They could use this "mountain" of suspicious evidence to fire you, and your only recourse would be to prove them wrong in a court or at a wrongful firing hearing. By then, your reputation would be trashed. Even if you won the hearing or trial, you wouldn't be exactly welcome back where you work, nor would any future potential employers be thrilled about hiring you.

Either way, you could find yourself standing on the unemployment line. You could be squeaky clean on your expenses, and they could suspect you of cheating. You could cheat like hell, and they could suspect you of cheating. If you are going to pay the piper, shouldn't you at least dance?

I can not and will not make this moral decision for you. I can not and will not be held responsible for what happens to you if you get caught. I will try to give you some guidelines as to what you can say if someone questions your expense report.

Deny, Deny, Deny, and Then Deny Again

The first and foremost rule about cheating on anything is to deny it until proven wrong. Once they prove you wrong, then you can move to another excuse. Even if someone else claims to know you are wrong, deny it. What makes their recollections any better than yours? I've always subscribed to the advice of a friend, "If they don't have videotape, they've got nothing."

Let's say your boss questions the number of miles you drove your car on a trip. They say, "It's only 150 miles from Gary to Indianapolis. Why are you claiming 500 miles for the round trip?"

You could say, "I don't know why, I just know what my odometer read before I started the trip and what it read when I got back, and that's what I turned in. I didn't watch every mile I drove."

If they push and say, "That's ridiculous. It's only 150 miles down I-65. Where did the extra miles come from?"

Let's look at the facts. Gary and Indianapolis, Indiana, are fairly large cities. From the south side of Gary to the north side of Indianapolis may be 150 miles. On the other hand, if you are going from the north side of Gary, to the south side of Indianapolis, the distance may be as much as 200 miles. Depending on situations and how many side trips you had to make while in the city, you could easily explain the difference with facts.

Here are some more creative excuses you might try to explain mileage differences.

"There was a big accident on I-65 and the police detoured us out in the country I don't how many miles."

"I got into Indianapolis and made a wrong turn on I-465 and did almost a complete loop around the city before I knew I was wrong."

"I made a wrong turn downtown trying to find the hotel and with all of those one way streets, I thought I'd never get there."

"I went to the Holiday Inn near the airport and then I found out I was supposed to be in the one by the Pyramids. That means I back tracked twice."

"Someone told me about a really great restaurant to try and it was a lot further away than the person told me it was. What was I supposed to do?"

If someone questions your facts, just remember to deny, deny, deny, and then deny again.

Switch To Another Set of Facts

Always take advantage of the time differential between when you take the trip, complete the expense report, turn it in, and when someone may question the details. Whenever you fill out an expense report with bogus or exaggerated data, you should always think of an excuse before you do it.

If you claim to be eating lunch with someone, you need to be prepared with an alternative answer if your boss knows for a fact you didn't. If you claim a twenty dollar cab fare when your boss knows the office is one block from the airport, you need to have an alternative.

You've got days to think about every intentional error you put on the report, while your boss has only seconds to respond to your excuse. There is no excuse for not being ready to respond.

Let's say you turn in a receipt for dinner. The blank tear off receipt you used was from some major national restaurant chain. You picked it up on another trip and saved it for later use. Your boss shows you the entry on the expense report and says, "I've been to this town just recently, and I don't remember there being one of these restaurants in town. What's going on here?"

You could try the denial excuse and it might go away. A better technique would be to switch the facts. Tell your boss, "I know, but I ate at this one place and got into an argument with the staff there and stormed out without remembering to get a receipt. After I got back to my hotel, I realized my mistake and I had this receipt sitting around, so I thought I'd use it. The amount is correct and I knew that accounts payable would need some kind of receipt, so I used it. I didn't think anyone would mind as long as the amount was correct. Was that okay?"

Your boss will probably buy it and at the most, tell you not to do it again. This possibility should tell you to survey restaurants in the town you visit. I make it a point to drive around the town for a few minutes, noting the names of restaurants, major intersections, shopping centers, and things like big factories. If your boss gets too nosy about where you ate or where you went, you can talk intelligently about the town. If you are lucky, you may even be able to trip your boss up, by knowing more about the town than they do.

I Have No Idea How That Happened

Depending on what item your boss is questions, you may want to try an excuse of total amazement. This is actually a variation on the denial. The difference is you are not denying what the boss is accusing. You are simply acknowledging their accusation, but being amazed at what has happened.

It may be easier to understand what I'm saying, by substituting an exaggerated conversation. You could imagine yourself saying, "I know what you think you see here. I can't see it, but if what you say is true, then I have no idea how that happened."

Let's say you reserved a hotel room at $50 a night, but you did either a rate switch trick or faked a receipt which actually shows $75 a night. Now let's say your boss somehow got a hold of your itinerary and it shows the reserved amount. When they come to accuse you of doing something wrong, take the two pieces of paper in your hand and say, "I see the reservation form and the receipt from the hotel. They must have messed up. I know this looks strange, but I honestly have no idea how this happened. If you want, you can approve the report as is. I'll call the hotel and try to get them to credit me. If they do, I'll deduct it from a future report."

Your boss likely feels comforted and validated, and will approve the report, and move on to Something else. The truth of the matter is, you will never call the hotel and never credit a future report. If the boss ever revisits this later, you simply say, "The hotel refused to do anything. So, I told them I will never stay there again and no one else in this company will either."

Challenge Your Boss As To Why They're Asking

Something I didn't tell you earlier in the book, about why your boss is not likely to check reports too closely, is a well kept secret. Your boss is probably also cheating on their expense report!

Within reason, your boss won't question expenses for concern someone will be alerted to a problem, audit everyone's expense reports and they'll be found out for padding their own reports. It is like the old proverb about throwing stones in glass houses.

From time to time, your boss may forget this, and in checking up on your expense report, you can remind them. You may even have a boss who believes it is okay to cheat on their own report, but they will not cut you any slack. That is an even better situation in which you should remind them.

Let me explain. You turn in a gasoline receipt for your rental car, where you've changed a two dollar slip into a twelve dollar slip by adding the extra one. If your boss comes in and accuses you of adding the one to cheat the company, you take the report and receipt in your hand and look at it for a minute or two.

You look at your boss with your best practiced indignant look and say, "I see what you are accusing me of. I'm not the kind of person who would ever have thought to try something like that. What made you think someone would do that? Have you ever done it?"

It sounds pretty strong, but the point is to divert attention away from the facts about the receipt. You need to get your boss off of accusing you about doing wrong, and get them defensive about accusing you of being a dishonest person at all.

The boss might get defensive, never wanting to admit why they thought of this cheating technique. They will also feel defensive for accusing you of cheating. Once you see they are on the defensive, you could go one step further and with a frustrated sigh, say, "Wow. I can't believe you thought I'd do something like that."

Chances are, your boss will drop the issue on the spot. They may even apologize for doubting you in the first place. If you listen closely, you may hear them say under their breath, "Sorry, but someone did this to me a long time ago, and I've been suspicious ever since."

If for some reason, it doesn't work, then you can switch over to another excuse mechanism. You may have to try the next one.

Offer To Take Back The Expense

If you press issues too hard, trying to legitimize a bogus expense, you run the risk of jeopardizing all of your future expense reports. This may be the time for a strategic retreat and offer to take the expense back.

The beauty of this trick, is you usually agree to give back nothing. If the receipt was totally fictitious, let's say for a meal you didn't eat, retracting the receipt costs you nothing. In exchange, you may completely shut down any future scrutiny. You need to weigh your position quickly and logically.

Let's go back to the receipt you turned in for the hotel rooms at $75 when they were actually only $50. If your boss is really digging in to the subject and you get the feeling they may call or write the hotel to get the duplicate records, you should regroup quickly.

Tell your boss, "You are right. It's my fault. I should have double checked the rate before I signed the bill. It isn't right for the company to pay the extra. I'll change my expense report and only charge the company for the $50 it should have been. I'll then deal with the hotel myself to get my own money back."

Your boss will likely respect your integrity and honesty, allow you make the changes, and let the issue drop. Monetarily you are out nothing, as the hotel room actually only cost you the fifty bucks. Strategically, you gained a great deal in lowering the suspicion level of your boss for future expense reports.

What To Do If You Get Caught Red Handed

No matter how good you are, you'll eventually make a mistake. No matter how careful you are, you will eventually forget some detail which will come back to haunt you. If you do this long enough and do it enough times, sooner or later, you're going to get caught.

It may take a long time. It depends upon how good you really are. I'm very, very good. If I weren't, I wouldn't be writing this book. I've never been caught, but I fully expect some day I will. When it happens, I will have to live with the consequences. If it happens to you, so must you.

One of the things I told you to do before trying any of the techniques in this book, is to weigh out the benefits of the extra income against the possible loss of your job. You can not have done it properly, unless you have reSolved yourself to the fact that you feel it is worth it. So, if you get caught, admit to it and throw yourself on the mercy of the court.

Let's say you turn in a receipt for a dinner with the purchasing agent of one of your customers. On the same night, your boss is having dinner with the same person, at the same restaurant you ate at with your spouse, and your boss saw you there. You're busted!

When your boss asks you about this one, you'll probably be called into their office and the door will be closed. They may ask you some coy question like, "How did the dinner with Bill Wilson go the other night?"

If your boss asks you a specific question after you turned in an expense report, alarm bells should go off in your head. Don't answer the question with anything else but another question. Your only response is, "Why do you ask?"

When your boss confronts you with the facts, admit to the crime. Do not admit to having ever done it before, no matter how hard your boss may press you. You simply say, "You got me. I knew you would, but I was short on money that week. I don't know why I did it. I gave in to temptation. I've never done it before, for fear of you catching me, and now that I've done it, I was right. I should have known better than to think I could get one by you.

What do we do now?"

If you have a great reputation, you may only get yelled at and told not to do it again, as "they" will be watching you. If you're reputation is okay, but not that wonderful, you are probably going to be written up and it will follow you around the remainder of your career with this company. If you are a marginal employee, they'll use it as an excuse to kick you out the door. All companies consider the "theft of company assets" as a major offense, worthy of immediate dismissal.

So, you can see now why planning your excuses before making entries on your expense report is so darned important. If you can't explain something to yourself before, how can you easily explain it to your boss after?

The damage to your life and your career, can be devastating if you get caught red-handed. This is a game of strategy. There have been a number of times where I wanted to cheat, but my gut told me the risks of being caught were too high. Pick and choose wisely where you cheat.

Paraphrasing an old proverb, "Those in doubt, who choose to run away, live to cheat another day."

Chapter Eight
A Few Final Words

Congratulations. By now your head is swimming with sinister ideas about padding your expense report, and you're asking yourself, "Why didn't I think of that?"

I'll tell you something really scary. This is just the tip of the ice berg. I've only shared with you what I consider "basic" techniques. If this book is a success, I may consider sharing the more advanced ones.

Even though these are the basic techniques, let me take a few pages here to examine just how much the typical business person stands to benefit from business travel and expense reports.

For this conversation, we will accept this business explorer makes twenty excursions each year which require carrier travel. This individual midpoints 3500 miles for each ticket to get there and back. This is generally among Chicago and Los Angeles full circle. The normal expense of each ticket to go full circle will be $1000.

This business explorer is as of now at the point level in their long standing customer club, where they are granted twofold focuses per mile flown. We'll additionally expect they visit two urban areas for every excursion, with each outing being Monday through Friday. They will lease a vehicle in every city for $45 per day for two days on each rental.

This individual will remain in inns four evenings each outing at a normal of $80 each night. In view of the change of towns and urban communities, and the accessibility of their lodging decision, this individual will just get inn accomplice miles with their carriers, at half of the stays.

This money manager eats genuine suppers, and purchases different dinners as diversion, at a normal of $200 per trip. A big part of these dinners are bought at cafés which take an interest in their charge card rebate

program.

Airline Points Earned By Traveling

The twenty excursions on the carrier, duplicated by the 3500 mile normal outing, is 70,000 genuine miles. This sum is multiplied to 140,000 as this individual has a place with the higher club level with the aircraft. Likewise, these projects have “level” grants at 30, 40, and 50,000 miles. For this explorer, they acquired a reward of 40,000 miles for the levels. The absolute miles acquired from the air travel for it is 180,000 miles.

By utilizing a rental vehicle organization which is joined forces with their aircraft regular customer program, this individual procures 500 focuses per rental when they show up on that carrier’s flight. On the twenty excursions, they lease vehicles multiple times. Increased by the 500 miles, they’ve acquired a reward of 20,000 miles.

This individual stays at taking part inns just 50% of the time, as their inn accomplice isn’t in each city, nor are they accessible 100% of the time. Thus, with 500 miles for every stay, this individual adds 10,000 miles per year to their program balance.

Likewise, they pay for these excursions on their charge card which acquires them miles on the aircraft. The charge card pays one point for every dollar went through, so the year’s charges could look like this:

Airline Tickets $1000 x 20 $20,000 Car Rentals $45 x 4 days x 20 $ 3,600 Hotel Room $80 x 4 days x 20 $ 6,400 Meals and Misc $200 x 20 $ 4,000 Personal Charges during the year $ 6,000

Total dollars charged $40,000 Therefore, the absolute carrier program miles procured for the extended period of voyaging would be:

Airline Miles Flown 70,000
Airline Club Level Bonus 70,000
Airline Plateau Awards 40,000
Charge Card Partner Miles 40,000
Rental Car Partner Miles 20,000
Hotel Partner Miles 10,000

Total Airline Frequent Flyer Points 250,000

By parlaying focuses from the accomplices in general, you’ve acquired a fourth of 1,000,000 aircraft miles in a single year, for flying just 70,000

genuine miles. In most carrier programs, 25,000 miles gets you a free ticket in the United States.
Using the equivalent $1000 normal cost for a ticket, as we utilized in the above models, your long standing customer focuses will get you ten free excursions with an absolute worth of $10,000.

On most projects, 40,000 miles gets you a free top of the line ticket in the United States. That would be approximately six tickets each year. If the average first class airline ticket is $3000, then your frequent flyer points would be worth
$18,000.

The harder things to esteem, are the extra coupons you get from the rental vehicle and inn accomplices who help out the carriers. Rental vehicle coupons can be utilized with the expectation of complimentary long stretches of rental, as a rule on a get one get one free premise, or moves up to higher vehicle rental classes for the whole rental. Lodging coupons may be with the expectation of complimentary evenings, marked down evenings, or redesigns, contingent on the inn network and the property at which you stay.

If you were simply ready to utilize them at the most reduced recovery rate, and you utilized them all, they would be esteemed at least $1500. Assuming you get a couple of breaks and extraordinary gives, you might get as much as $3000. I

Actual Dollars Earned On Your Expense Reports

For this model, I will accept somebody being really forceful at applying the standards in this book. This will by no means be the most you can get. I will utilize similar voyager and conditions we utilized in the carrier miles model. This individual will be really forceful, however they will not be pushing it.

If you are somebody who flies considerably more and needs to face more challenges on each cost report, you can take significantly bigger measures of money. The twenty excursion each year explorer is likely nearer to the normal, and even with a normal utilization of the cushioning standards, I think you'll be enjoyably astonished by how much cash you can get.

One individual stays at inns with free breakfast and party time snacks, so they will add $30 each day in invented individual suppers. They will add $20 per trip in swelled gas charges, costs, and stopping .

Using coupons, making plan changes, and slashing prevents from their aircraft tickets, this individual will average $50 per ticket of expanded charges on a cost report. By turning the arms and rules of the lodgings in which they stay, this explorer will gather $5 each day in false or swelled expenses.

Moreover, this voyager will discount imaginary or raised charges for amusement in how much $50 per trip. At long last, of the $4000 of individual dinners and diversion for which this explorer really paid, half were at eateries which refund 20% through their charge card.

The last thing to consider is the expense investment funds to you of voyaging. Assuming you are out and about, you are not paying for dinners you would typically eat at

home. You are not bringing about significant distance telephone charges. You are not running your water radiator, heater, TV, oven, or other utility things however much you would on the off chance that you had been home.

When everything is added up to, this could undoubtedly be $25 a day you've saved. The cash you didn't need to spend on day by day everyday costs, is equivalent to additional money in your pocket.

Always remember the coincidental advantage of living for nothing on the organization, when going on business. The yearly sum this representative will gather from their cost report in genuine money, could be:

Meals

Gas

Airline

Hotel

Entertain. Rebate

Personal $30 day x 4 days x 20 outings $2,400 $20 trip x 20 outings $ 400 $50 trip x 20 outings $1,000 $5 day x 4 days x 20 outings $ 400 $50 trip x 20 outings $1,000 20% x half x $4,000 $ 400 $25 day x 4 days x 20 excursions $2,000

Total Cash Generated On Expense Reports $7,600

If you were this business explorer, you just gave yourself a money raise of

$7,600 over your ordinary salary. That is more than $600 every month. Since it is money or salary, you need to figure in the ordinary expenses. For the majority of us, this expansion would have been more than $12,500 before charges. You have provided yourself with a raise of $1,000 per month without working any harder.

What's The Total Benefit?

Well, we should see. This individual got at least $10,000 in carrier tickets by effectively augmenting their long standing customer program benefits. They got at least $1500 in lodging and rental vehicle benefits. They likewise got $7600 in hard virus cash. According to my observations, that is a base advantage of over

$19,000.

Since this is bring home or net cash, missing duties, we want to sort out what the pre-charge sum would be. At the point when you figure the normal duty rate, you'll observe these strategies can provide you with a compelling individual raise of over
$31,800.

What this means to you is a superior, or possibly a more well-to-do seeming way of life. In the event that this individual made $50,000 every year, they can carry on with the way of life of somebody making $80,000 per year. Any way you may decide to support it.

The advantages can be substantial.

Some Words Of Advice

I need to allow you one last opportunity to rethink whether you heed the guidance in this book. It is illicit and untrustworthy to undermine your cost report. Assuming you in all actuality do get found out, you could get terminated or shipped off jail.

On the other hand, if your supervisor needs to lessen expenses to make their benefit numbers, ensure their own reward, or in any capacity get what they need, you could be an ideal worker and wind up kicked out the door.

If you truly do get found out and they fire you, take steps to sue. Tell them, as a feature of the preliminary revelation, you will request cost report duplicates from every one of the top leaders to check whether they cheated.

As a last suggestion, "Relax, your manager is most likely undermining their cost report too."

One Final Postscript

There is no question you purchased this book to perceive how to cushion your own cost report and pull off it. Chances are, assuming your manager saw this book, they got it also, for exactly the same reasons.

This book is a two way road and a double sided deal. It tells you the best way to undermine your costs, however it additionally illuminates you regarding ways your own workers are attempting to undermine their cost reports.

No one would purchase a book called, "How To Catch Employees Who Cheat On Their Expense Reports...", yet this book can and will be utilized in that way.

If this book turns out to be hugely famous and great many individuals read it, there will be a fascinating little conflict happening in the business world. It'll be a conflict between the people who read it against the individuals who have not. I consider myself to be an arms provider to the two sides of the fight.

Friends who have reviewed this book have asked me, "Don't you feel regretful empowering those individuals to undermine their expenses?" My reaction is, "They as of now are!"

www.ingramcontent.com/pod-product-compliance
Lightning Source LLC
LaVergne TN
LVHW090138160826
845673LV00017B/2505

* 9 7 9 8 4 1 7 9 9 6 0 9 2 *